Cambridge Certificate in Advanced English 6

WITH ANSWERS

Examination papers from University of Cambridge ESOL Examinations: English for Speakers of Other Languages

CAMBRIDGE
UNIVERSITY PRESS

CAMBRIDGE UNIVERSITY PRESS
Cambridge, New York, Melbourne, Madrid, Cape Town, Singapore, São Paulo

Cambridge University Press
The Edinburgh Building, Cambridge CB2 8RU, UK

www.cambridge.org
Information on this title: www.cambridge.org/9780521613736

First published 2005
3rd printing 2007

Printed in the United Kingdom at the University Press, Cambridge

A catalogue record for this publication is available from the British Library

ISBN 978-0-521-61372-9 Student's Book
ISBN 978-0-521-61373-6 Student's Book with answers
ISBN 978-0-521-61376-7 Cassette Set
ISBN 978-0-521-61377-4 Audio CD Set
ISBN 978-0-521-61374-3 Self-study Pack

Contents

Thanks and acknowledgements

The publishers are grateful to the following for permission to use copyright material. Whilst every effort has been made to locate the owners of the copyright, in some cases this has been unsuccessful. The publishers apologise for any infringement or failure to acknowledge the original sources and will be glad to include any necessary correction in subsequent printings.

The Independent for the extract on pp.10–11 from 'How I built the boat of my dreams' by Tom Cunliffe, and for the adapted article on p.40 from 'The Tartan Machine' by Sally Varlow © Independent News & Media (UK) Ltd, 1999; *The Sunday Telegraph* for the text on pp.15–16 from 'Departure Points' by Tim Pozzi © Telegraph Group Limited, 1 November 1998; *BBC Wildlife Magazine* for the adapted extracts on p.37 from 'Natural Classic' book reviews © Origin Publishing Ltd, *The Times* for the adapted text on p.38–39 from 'In search of true north' by Anjana Ahuja © Times Newspapers Ltd, 1997; for the extract on p. 65 from *Working with Emotional Intelligence* by Daniel Goleman, © 1998 by Daniel Goleman. Used by permission of Bantam Books, a division of Random House and Bloomsbury Publishing Plc; *The Telegraph* for the extract on p.66–67 from 'Beginner takes all' by Serena Allott © Telegraph Group Limited, 1998; Georgina Ferry for the adapted text on pp.71–72 from 'Dorothy Who?', published in *The Financial Times*, 5/6 December 1998; Roger Bray for the extract on pp.94–95 adapted from 'Where the landscape will do the walking' published in *The Financial Times*, 1999.

For permission to reproduce copyright photographs:

C1: © Keren Su/Corbis, *centre*; © Peter Turnley/Corbis, *bottom right*; Photos for Books/photographersdirect.com, *top right*; Image Source/Rex Features, *top left*; Peter Frischmuth/Still Pictures, *bottom left*.
C2: Topfoto/The Image Works, *top left*; Hugh Penney Photography/photographersdirect.com, *top right*; Getty Images, *bottom left & right*;
C3: © Gary Houlder/Corbis, *top*; © Michael S. Yamashita/Corbis, centre; Getty Images, *bottom*.
C4: © Little Blue Wolf Productions/Corbis, *bottom left*; Kayte Deioma/photographersdirect.com, *top*; Getty Images, *centre left & bottom right*; Brad Mitchell Photography/photographersdirect.com, *centre right*.
C5: © Jonathan Blair/Corbis, *top*; Topfoto, *bottom*.
C7: © Royalty Free/Corbis, *centre right*; Education Photos/John Walmsley, *bottom right*; Getty Images, *top & centre left*; Topfoto/The Image Works, *bottom left*.
C8: © Royalty Free/Corbis, *top*; Empics/SportsChrome, *bottom*.
C9: Leslie Garland Picture Library/Alamy, *top left*; Chris Howes/Wild Places Photography/Alamy, *bottom right*; Empics/AP, *top right*; Volvox/Robert Harding Picture Library, *centre left*; Rex Features, *bottom left*.
C10: © Robert Holmes/Corbis, *top*; Getty Images, *bottom*.
C12: Photograph by James Veysey/Camera Press London, *lower centre*; Getty Images, *upper centre*; Imagestate, *bottom*; Rob van Nostrand, PerfectPhoto, CA/photographersdirect.com, *top*.
C13: © John Angerson, *bottom left & right*; Seandrakes/photographersdirect.com, *top right*; Jacky Chapman/Photofusion/photographersdirect.com, *top left*.
C14: Photograph by James Veysey/Camera Press London, *upper centre*; Getty Images, *lower centre*; Imagestate, *top*; Rob van Nostrand, PerfectPhoto, CA/photographersdirect.com, *bottom*.
C15: A1PIX/GrandAngleFoto/photographersdirect.com, *top left*; Empics/AP, *centre right & bottom left*; EDP Pics/K.Tovell/Rex Features, *centre left*; Topfoto/The Image Works, *top right & bottom right*.
C16: © John Angerson, *top left & right*; Seandrakes/photographersdirect.com, *bottom left*; Jacky Chapman/Photofusion/photographersdirect.com, *bottom right*.

Artwork: Servis Filmsetting Limited

Picture research by Sandie Huskinson-Rolfe of PHOTOSEEKERS

Design concept by Peter Ducker

Cover design by Dunne & Scully

The recordings which accompany this book were made at Studio AVP, London.

Introduction

This collection of four complete practice tests comprises past papers from the University of Cambridge ESOL Examinations Certificate in Advanced English (CAE) examination; students can practise these tests on their own or with the help of a teacher.

The CAE examination is part of a group of examinations developed by Cambridge ESOL called the Cambridge Main Suite. The Main Suite consists of five examinations that have similar characteristics but are designed for different levels of English language ability. Within the five levels, CAE is at Level C1 in the *Council of Europe's Common European Framework of Reference for Languages: Learning, teaching, assessment.* It has also been accredited by the Qualifications and Curriculum Authority in the UK as a Level 2 ESOL certificate in the National Qualifications Framework. The CAE examination is widely recognised in commerce and industry and in individual university faculties and other educational institutions.

Examination	Council of Europe Framework Level	UK National Qualifications Framework Level
CPE Certificate of Proficiency in English	C2	3
CAE Certificate in Advanced English	C1	2
FCE First Certificate in English	B2	1
PET Preliminary English Test	B1	Entry 3
KET Key English Test	A2	Entry 2

Further information

The information contained in this practice book is designed to be an overview of the exam. For a full description of all of the above exams including information about task types, testing focus and preparation, please see the relevant handbooks which can be obtained from Cambridge ESOL at the address below or from the website at: www.CambridgeESOL.org

University of Cambridge ESOL Examinations
1 Hills Road
Cambridge CB1 2EU
United Kingdom

Telephone: +44 1223 553355
Fax: +44 1223 460278
e-mail: ESOLHelpdesk@ucles.org.uk

The structure of CAE: an overview

The CAE examination consists of five papers.

Paper 1   Reading   1 hour 15 minutes
This paper consists of **four** parts, each containing one text or several shorter pieces. There are between 40 and 50 multiple-matching, multiple-choice and gapped-text questions in total.

Paper 2   Writing   2 hours
This paper consists of **two** parts and candidates have to complete two tasks (letters, reports, articles, competition entries, proposals, reviews and leaflets) of approximately 250 words each. **Part 1** consists of one compulsory task based on substantial reading input. **Part 2** consists of one task selected from a choice of four. Question 5 is always related to business.

Paper 3   English in Use   1 hour 30 minutes
This paper consists of **six** parts, designed to test the ability to apply knowledge of the language system, including vocabulary, grammar, spelling and punctuation, word-building, register and cohesion. It contains **80** items in total.

Paper 4   Listening   45 minutes (approximately)
This paper consists of **four** parts, each with texts of varying length and nature which test a wide range of listening skills. There are between 30 and 40 sentence completion, note completion, multiple-choice and multiple-matching questions in total. Parts 1, 3 and 4 are heard twice whereas Part 2 is heard only once.

Paper 5   Speaking   15 minutes
This paper consists of **four** parts, based on visual stimuli and verbal prompts. Candidates are examined in pairs by two examiners, one taking the part of the interlocutor and the other of the assessor.

Candidates are assessed individually. The assessor focuses on grammar and vocabulary, discourse management, pronunciation, and interactive communication. The interlocutor provides a global mark for the whole test.

Grading

The overall CAE grade is based on the total score gained in all five papers. It is not necessary to achieve a satisfactory level in all five papers in order to pass the examination. Certificates are given to candidates who pass the examination with grade A, B or C. A is the highest. The minimum successful performance in order to achieve grade C corresponds to about 60% of the total marks. D and E are failing grades. All candidates are sent a Statement of Results which includes a graphical profile of their performance in each paper and shows their relative performance in each one. Each paper is weighted to 40 marks. Therefore, the five CAE papers total 200 marks, after weighting.

For further information on grading and results, go to the website (see page 5).

Test 1

PAPER 1   READING (1 hour 15 minutes)

Part 1

Answer questions **1–16** by referring to the newspaper article about clock radios on page **9**. Indicate your answers **on the separate answer sheet**.

For questions **1–16**, answer by choosing from the sections of the article (**A–E**) on page 9. Some of the choices may be required more than once.

In which section are the following mentioned?

a tester admitting that he did not trust any type of alarm clock	1.....A....
a tester later regretting having touched the controls	2.....B....
a tester approving of a model because of its conspicuous appearance	3.....D....
the testers being able to operate the model without reference to the manual	4....D....
a tester's praise for a model despite the existence of a technical fault	B ✗ 5..E....
doubts about the reliability of a model because of the design of an additional feature	6........C
the testers feeling positive about their success in getting the model to work	B ✗ 7...E...
doubts about whether anyone would wish to follow certain instructions from the manual	8..A....
an explanation of why companies had started to make better radios	9..E.....
the intended market for the model being apparent from its design	10..D.....
a tester realising that he had drawn the wrong conclusion about a particular feature	A ✓ 11....B.....
the testers agreeing on the usefulness of a particular feature	B ✗12..C.....
an additional feature which made the price seem competitive	13..A....
uncertainty over whether the radio controls had been set in the correct sequence	E ✗ 14..C.....
a tester's reaction to the imprecision of the alarm	15...D....
surprise at the commercial success of a particular model	16..C.....

11 / 16.

SOUND THE ALARM
Stuart Harris reports

Many of us listen to the radio when we get up in the morning and most of us also require some external means to persuade us to get out of bed. Thus we have the clock radio. But how do you pick a good one? Our panel, which consisted of myself plus the inventor Tom Granger and the broadcaster Paul Bridges, tested five currently available.

A

The 'dual alarm function' that is advertised with this model does not allow you, as I first supposed, to be woken by the buzzer, snooze a while and then finally be driven out of bed. The instruction booklet advises you to use this function to set two different wake-up times, one for work days and one for weekends, but whose life is programmed to this extent?

Since this model costs more or less the same as the second model tested, the inclusion of a cassette player is quite a bargain – you can fall asleep to your own soothing tapes and wake up to a day without news. We all thought the quality of the radio excellent, too – if only the whole thing was smaller. It's as big as a rugby ball. Paul Bridges said, 'Any clock radio I buy has to leave enough space on the bedside table for my keys, wallet, glasses and telephone. Anyway, I'm completely paranoid and always book a wake-up call in case the alarm doesn't go off.'

B

This model was voted best in the beauty stakes and overall winner. Paul Bridges declared himself 'in love with it', although the clock on the one he tested 'kept getting stuck at 16.00'. I was fascinated by the digital display, with its classy grey numbers on a gentle green background. The wide snooze bar means you can tap it on the edge with your eyes shut. Unfortunately, the smooth undulations and tactile buttons, like pebbles on the beach, encouraged me to run my fingers over them as if they were keys on a piano, which proved my undoing when I finally looked at the 80-page instruction booklet.

The clock has a self-power back-up so you don't have to reset it if someone unceremoniously pulls the plug out in order to use a hairdryer or the vacuum cleaner; this met with unanimous approval. However, we all found it a technical feat to set up – though completing the learning curve made us feel 'cool' and sophisticated.

C

Tom Granger described this model with its extra built-in lamp as 'unbelievably tacky' in the way it's made. 'You have to wrench the funny light out of its socket to get it to work, which makes me wonder about the quality of the rest of it.' He complained that he had to read the instruction booklet twice before he could get it to work; the clock kept leaping from 12.00 to 02.00 so he had to go round again.

The light was certainly hard to position; you would never be able to read by it – it only shines on the clock, which is illuminated anyway. Paul Bridges said he was 'very tickled' by the lamp idea but agreed that the radio was hard to tune. The buzzer is reminiscent of 'action stations' on a submarine and made me feel like hurling the whole thing across the bedroom. Interestingly, however, this model is the third most popular on the market.

D

Clearly aimed at young people, with its brightly coloured casing and matching bootlace strap, this one appealed to the child in Tom Granger and me. 'I would choose this one because it doesn't disappear into the background like the others,' he said. In fact, the traditional design of the controls made it the only one we managed to set up without reading the instruction booklet. Too bad the alarm is allowed a hilarious 20-minute margin for error; the manual notes, 'the alarm may sound about 10 minutes earlier or later than the pre-set time'. Paul Bridges scoffed at such a notion, adding that this model was 'terribly fiddly' and, indeed, 'completely useless'.

E

The simplest and cheapest of all the models tested, this scored points with Tom Granger because it 'seemed very standard and took up little space', but also because it has old-fashioned dial tuning. 'It's more intuitive to set up. With modern push-button tuning you're never really sure if you've pressed all the buttons in the right order so you can't have confidence that the thing will actually work.' He accepted, however, that manufacturers had been obliged to improve the quality of radios because of the advent of button-tuning. I thought the tuning rather crude, as did Paul Bridges, but we agreed that the radio quality was fine. The buzzer on this model certainly works; it succeeded in getting me out of bed in just two beeps!

Part 2

For questions **17–22**, you must choose which of the paragraphs **A–G** on page **11** fit into the numbered gaps in the following magazine article. There is one extra paragraph which does not fit in any of the gaps. Indicate your answers **on the separate answer sheet**.

THE BOAT OF MY DREAMS

The best boat design should combine old and new, says Tom Cunliffe. And he put it into practice in his own craft, 'The Westerman'.

This week, the Summer Boat Show in London is resplendent with fine yachts, bristling with new technology. Nearly all are descendants of the hull-shape revolution that took place 25 years ago. By contrast, my own lies quietly on a tidal creek off the south coast. She was designed last year but, seeing her, you might imagine her to be 100 years old and think that her owner must be some kind of lost-soul romantic.

17	G x F

It has to be said, however, that despite being an indispensable tool in current design methods and boat-building practice, sophisticated technology frequently insulates crews from the harsh realities of maritime life. These are often the very realities they hoped to rediscover by going to sea in the first place.

18	A

The occasional battle with flapping canvas is surely part of a seaman's life. And for what purpose should we abandon common sense and move our steering positions from the security of the aft end to some vulnerable perch half-way to the bow? The sad answer is that this creates a cabin like that of an ocean liner, with space for a bed larger than the one at home.

19	G

Her sails were heavy, and she had no pumped water, no electricity to speak of, no fridge, no central heating, no winches, and absolutely no electronics, especially in the navigation department, yet she was the kindest, easiest boat that I have ever sailed at sea.

20	E x B

The Westerman has never disappointed me. Although Nigel Irens, the designer, and Ed Burnett, his right-hand man, are adept with computer-assisted design programs, Irens initially drew this boat on a paper napkin, and only later transferred his ideas to the computer. After this had generated a set of lines, he carved a model, just as boatyards did in the days of sail. Together we considered the primary embryonic vessel, then fed the design back into the electronic box for modification.

21	D

Her appearance is ageless, her motion at sea is a pleasure and her accommodation, much of it in reclaimed pitch pine, emanates an atmosphere of deep peace. Maybe this is because she was drawn purely as a sailing craft, without reference to any furniture we might put into her. That is the well-tried method of the sea.

22   B x C

Constructed in timber treated with a penetrating glue, she is totally impervious to water. Thus she has all the benefits of a glass fibre boat yet looks like, feels like and sails like the real thing.

A   It's not that I'm suggesting that sailors should go back to enduring every hardship. It's always been important to me that my boats have a coal stove for warmth and dryness and cosy berths for sleeping. But why go cruising at all if every sail sets and furls itself?

B   Back on land, however, it is a sad fact that the very antiquity of classic boats means that they need a lot of looking after. When I had a bad injury to my back, I realised that my 15-year love affair with her had to end. Searching for a younger replacement produced no credible contenders, so I decided to build a new boat from scratch.

C   In her timeless serenity, she is the living proof that it works; that there is no need to follow current fashions to find satisfaction, and that sometimes it pays to listen to the lessons of history.

D   The next version was nearly right and by the time the final one appeared, the form was perfect. The completed boat has now crossed the North Atlantic and has won four out of her first six racing starts.

E   At the same time, having lived aboard an ancient wooden beauty in the early seventies, it's easier to understand more of this area of the mechanics. My designer, for example, knows more about the ways of a boat on the sea than anyone I can think of.

F   Perhaps I am, though I doubt it. This boat has benefited from all the magic of old-fashioned boat design, but it would have been a much harder job without the advances of modern know-how.

G   For me a boat should always be a boat and not a cottage on the water. When I bought an earlier boat, *Hirta*, in which I circumnavigated Britain for a TV race series, the previous owner observed that she had every comfort, but no luxury. During my long relationship with her, *Hirta* taught me how wise he was.

New horizons: Tom Cunliffe on board 'The Westerman'

Part 3

Read the following magazine article and answer questions **23–27** on page **13**. **On your answer sheet**, indicate the letter **A**, **B**, **C** or **D** against the number of each question, **23–27**. Give only one answer to each question.

Margaret and her liquid assets

Margaret Wilkins is said to have a 'sixth sense'. She can hold a forked hazel rod above the ground and detect water. She is increasingly in demand by farmers whose wells have dried up.

Together with her husband, Margaret Wilkins runs a well-drilling business, using technology such as drilling rigs and air-compressed hammers. But when it comes to locating water, she needs nothing more than a forked hazel stick. The couple's success rate is higher than 90 per cent. Dowsing – the ability to locate water, minerals and lost objects underground – is a so-called 'sixth sense'. There are many theories about how it is done, ranging from the physical, such as magnetism, to the spiritual. One of the most credible is based on the knowledge that everything on this planet vibrates, water more than other matter. It is suggested that dowsers have an acute ability to sense vibrations while standing on the Earth's surface; some dowsers say that they can 'sense' water, others that they can smell it, smell being the most acute sense.

For the Wilkins, the drought years of recent times have been busy, with an almost six-week-long waiting list at one stage. Most of Margaret's customers are farmers with wells that have dried up: 'We will see customers only once in a lifetime because wells last for a long time.' Other customers own remote cottages or barns, now holiday homes, where the expense of running water pipes for great distances is prohibitive. Others are golf-course developers with clubhouse facilities to build.

Margaret tries to locate water between 50 and 70 metres down. 'You can't drill a well where there is the slightest risk of farm or other waste getting into the water supply. The water we locate is running in fissures of impervious rock and, as long as we bring the water straight up, it should give a good clean supply, though Cornwall is rich in minerals so you have to watch out for iron.'

Another necessity is electricity to drive the pump; this is too expensive to run across miles of fields so ideally the well should be near to existing power supplies.

After considering all this, Margaret can start to look for water. On large areas, such as golf courses, she begins with a map of the area and a pendulum. 'I hold the pendulum still and gently move it over the map. It will swing when it is suspended over an area where there is water.'

After the map has indicated likely areas, Margaret walks over the fields with a hazel stick, forked and equal in length and width each side. 'Once I'm above water I get a peculiar feeling; I reel slightly. When it subsides I use the stick to locate the exact spot where we should drill.' Gripping the two forks of the stick with both hands, she eases them outwards slightly to give tension. 'When water is immediately below, the straight part of the stick rises up. It's vital to drill exactly where the stick says. A fraction the wrong way, and you can miss the waterline altogether. My husband will dowse the same area as me; usually, not always, we agree on the precise place to drill. If we disagree, we won't drill and will keep looking until we do agree.'

Margaret Wilkins is not in isolation, carrying out some curious old tradition down in the west of England. Anthropologists and writers have long been fascinated by this inexplicable intuition. Margaret calls it an 'intuitive perception of the environment' and that is the closest we can get to understanding why she locates water so accurately. If she did not have this 'sixth sense', how else could the family live off their well-drilling business year after year?

23 What does the writer say about the theory of vibration and dowsers?

    A It has only recently been accepted.
    B There are limits to its application.
    C There might be some truth in it.
    D It is based on inaccurate information.

24 One reason why people employ Margaret to find water is

    A the isolated position of their property.
    B the failure of their own efforts.
    C the low fees she charges for her work.
    D the speed at which she operates.

25 Margaret is cautious about new finds of water in Cornwall because they may be

    A unfit for human consumption.
    B too insignificant to be worthwhile.
    C too deep to bring to the surface.
    D expensive to locate with certainty.

26 When Margaret and her husband use the dowsing stick to locate places to drill, they

    A are unlikely to achieve the same result.
    B have regular differences of opinion.
    C employ different techniques.
    D are unwilling to take risks.

27 What does the writer suggest as proof of the effectiveness of Margaret's dowsing?

    A the interest shown in it by anthropologists and writers
    B the regular income which can be made from it
    C people's appreciation of the tradition behind it
    D people's description of it as a 'sixth sense'

Part 4

Answer questions **28–46** by referring to the newspaper article on pages **15–16** about giving up work to go travelling. Indicate your answers **on the separate answer sheet**.

For questions **28–46**, answer by choosing from the sections of the article (**A–E**). Some of the choices may be required more than once.

Note: When more than one choice is required, these may be given **in any order**.

In which section(s) of the article are the following mentioned?

the view that going travelling does not represent escaping from something	**28**..........	
a belief that going travelling provides a last opportunity for fun before leading a more conventional life	**29**..........	
anxiety as to how to deal with a practical issue	**30**..........	
the feeling experienced immediately after giving up a job	**31**..........	**32**..........
regret at not having gone travelling	**33**..........	
a feeling that the desire to travel may indicate immaturity	**34**..........	
a feeling that older people may not fit in with other travellers	**35**..........	
delaying the date of departure of a journey	**36**..........	
a feeling shared by everybody who goes travelling later in life	**37**..........	
losing self-respect by remaining in a job	**38**..........	
considering the effect of going travelling on career prospects	**39**..........	
the attitude of some employers to employees who go travelling	**40**..........	
a belief that going travelling may result in greater flexibility as a person	**41**..........	
the personal qualities required in order to decide to go travelling	**42**..........	
the knowledge that permanent employment has become less usual	**43**..........	
changes in life that prevent people from going travelling	**44**..........	
having no strong desires professionally	**45**..........	
looking forward more and more to going travelling	**46**..........	

I may be too old for this lark, but here goes!

At 34, Tim Pozzi has left a good job to go backpacking. He ponders what has made him – and others of his age – take the plunge.

A

This summer, I quit my job and resolved to rent out my flat and go travelling in South East Asia for a year. You might think I'm lucky, but I'm 34 years old, and I'm nervous.

It's not as if I haven't done the travelling thing before. After university, I spent two years backpacking around North and South America, and when I returned, was determined to do it again some day. But you know how it is ... I fell in love, embarked on a career, bought a flat and got used to earning a salary. But I gradually realised I had been sacrificing my own sense of worth for my salary. When I handed in that letter of resignation, it felt as though I'd taken charge of my life again.

I now have no ties. Many of my friends are now married with children and, while they wouldn't swap places with me, they envy me my lack of responsibilities. I'm no longer in a relationship, and I have no burning career ambitions. I feel almost obliged to make the most of that freedom – if only for my friends' sake!

B

Why am I so nervous? In the first place, it's a question of making the necessary arrangements. How could I bear to have someone else living in my home? And how would I go about organising the letting? And apart from anything else, I had to decide where to go.

I'm a shocking procrastinator, and am already several weeks behind my intended schedule. 'Might as well enjoy the summer in England,' I told myself. Then, 'Why not hang around for the start of the football season?' Severing emotional ties makes it even more difficult.

I'm putting it off because, deep down, I wonder if I can still cope with backpacking. Will I be able to readjust to a more basic way of life? Will I feel out of place among a community of backpackers fresh out of school and university?

Perhaps not. I've discovered it's increasingly common for Britons in their late twenties and thirties to want to disentangle themselves from the lives they've made for themselves and head off for foreign climes.

C

Jennifer Cox, of *Lonely Planet* guidebook publishers, identifies a growing awareness that adventure is there for the taking: 'The penny's dropped. The sort of people who always say "I wish I'd had that opportunity" are realising that they can have it any time they want. They just have to be brave enough and organised enough and confident enough to do it.'

For Danny, a 30-year-old accountant, and his girlfriend Tammy, a 28-year-old teacher, it's a chance to have a final fling before settling down. They have bought a round-the-world ticket for a year. 'I'm prepared to sacrifice job security to have the trip,' says Danny. 'There's always a niggling thought at the back of your mind that, "OK, I'm not moving up the career ladder, I'm going to be in the same position I was in before when I come back," but I think it's a risk you have to take. When I left the office, I threw my calculator into the river as a ceremonial act of defiance!'

For Matt, who'd just got out of the Army, the year he spent travelling amounted to a period of metamorphosis. 'When you're in the military, there's a set way of doing things, a pattern to the way you approach problems. I went away because I really needed to temper this, and get rid of this approach in some cases, in order to have a reasonable existence as a civilian.'

D

While there are as many reasons to go travelling at my time of life as there are travellers, there do seem to be common factors. 'We have a much more flexible workforce today,' says Angela Baron of the Institute of Personnel Development. 'There are more people working on short-term contracts and so if your contract's just come to an end you've got nothing to lose.' Larger companies are even adopting career-break policies. 'If you've spent a lot of time and money training someone, it's nice to know they're coming back at some point rather than going to work for a competitor.'

For Dan Hiscocks, managing director of Travellerseye, a publishing company that specialises in the tales of 'ordinary' travellers, an increasing number of thirty-somethings are taking stock of their lives. 'If you're not happy doing what you're doing – and many people aren't – it's no longer a question of just seeing it through. Now people are aware that opportunities exist and that a job isn't "for life" any more. Travel offers a chance to reassess, to take a step back and think about your life.'

E

Is giving in to wanderlust just another example of my generation's inability to come to terms with adulthood? Jennifer Cox thinks not. 'It's a sign of a better educated, more stable society when we're less concerned with paying the bills than wanting to live a balanced life. We're actually taking the time to ask "Is this what I want?"'

Ben, a 32-year-old picture researcher heading off to Central America for a year, does not believe he's running away. 'It's more a case of running towards something. It's trying to grab some things that I want for myself.' But he does feel some trepidation. 'It's the thought of what I'm leaving behind, that comfortable routine – just the act of going into the office every day, saying "hi" to everyone and sitting down with a cup of coffee.'

I share Ben's reservations about leaving behind an ordered life with few challenges and I'm not sure I'd be making this journey if I hadn't found my boss intolerable. As Jennifer Cox points out: 'This is fairly typical. There's often a catalyst, like the break-up of a relationship or the loss of a job. Such an event can push people to go and do it.'

It may have taken a helpful kick up the backside to get me moving, but I'm now approaching the next 12 months with a mounting sense of excitement. Whatever the outcome, I'll be able to take satisfaction in having grabbed life by the horns. And in that I'm sure I speak for all of us ageing backpackers.

PAPER 2 WRITING (2 hours)

Part 1

1   You are studying at a college in Fordham in England. Fordham town council has decided to turn Greendale Park, which is opposite your college, into a car park. After reading an article in the local newspaper about this, your class conducted interviews and did a survey among residents in the town. You have decided to write a letter to the editor of the newspaper.

Read the newspaper article and look at the chart below, together with the comments from Fordham residents on page **18**. Then, **using the information appropriately**, write the letter to the editor, responding to the article, briefly summarising the information from the survey and presenting your conclusions.

Council Sees Sense

The town council has at last decided to do something about the problem of parking in Fordham. Greendale Park is to become a large car park, with spaces for 800 cars.

This newspaper is fully in favour of turning what is a little-used area into something which will really help this town. We think that money will be better spent on easing the town's parking problems, rather than on looking after flowers and tennis courts!

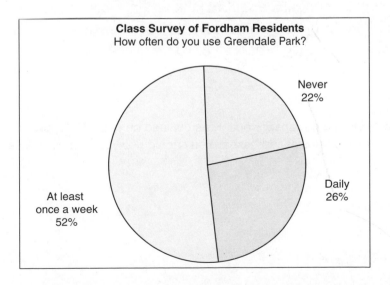

Class Survey of Fordham Residents
How often do you use Greendale Park?

Never 22%

Daily 26%

At least once a week 52%

Typical comments from Fordham residents

I usually go into the park to eat my lunch – it makes a nice change from being in the office all day. It's good to have some fresh air in the town.

I often take my grandchildren into the park to run around and play on the swings. Kids don't have anywhere else round here to play safely.

It's really great going to play tennis in the park in the summer. The only other place to go is to a private tennis club and we can't afford that. The courts in the park are good value.

I think the council should think again. How about building an underground car park or knocking down the empty factory near the river?

Now write your **letter** to the newspaper editor, as outlined on page **17** (approximately 250 words). You do not need to include postal addresses. You should use your own words as far as possible.

Part 2

Choose **one** of the following writing tasks. Your answer should follow exactly the instructions given. Write approximately 250 words.

2   You read the following announcement in **Sports Watch**, a sports magazine.

> We are conducting an international survey on sports and would like to publish readers' articles which tell us about **both** of the following points:
> • Which **two** sports do you most enjoy watching, and why?
> • Do you think sports in your country have been influenced by sports from abroad? Why do you think this is the case?

Write your **article**.

3   You see the following announcement for a competition in an international magazine.

> # TIME CAPSULE – TO BE OPENED IN 100 YEARS' TIME!
>
> We are preparing a special container designed to be buried underground and opened in 100 years' time. We invite our readers to recommend **three** things to include in this time capsule which represent life and culture today, and to say why they would be of interest to people in the future.

Write your **competition entry**.

4   An international research group is investigating attitudes to education in different parts of the world. You have been asked to write a report on education in your country. Your report should address the following questions:
• What are the strengths and weaknesses of education in your country?
• What educational developments would you like to see in your country in the future?

Write your **report**.

5   The company you work for is keen to promote international business contacts. Consequently, your department is allowed to send employees abroad to work in foreign companies for up to three months. You would like to do this, so your head of department has asked you to submit a proposal to him. The proposal must explain:
• which type of foreign company you would like to work in, and why
• what you would like to do at this foreign company
• how your visit will benefit the company you now work for.

Write your **proposal**.

PAPER 3   ENGLISH IN USE (1 hour 30 minutes)

Part 1

For questions **1–15**, read the text below and then decide which answer on page **21** best fits each space. Indicate your answer **on the separate answer sheet**. The exercise begins with an example **(0)**.

Example:

The early railway in Britain

In 1830, there were under 100 miles of public railway in Britain. Yet within 20 years, this **(0)** ..... had grown to more than 5,000 miles. By the end of the century, almost enough rail track to **(1)** ..... the world covered this small island, **(2)** ..... the nature of travel for ever and contributing to the industrial revolution that changed the **(3)** ..... of history in many parts of the world.

   Wherever railways were introduced, economic and social progress quickly **(4)** ..... . In a single day, rail passengers could travel hundreds of miles, **(5)** ..... previous journey times by huge margins and bringing rapid travel within the **(6)** ..... of ordinary people. Previously, many people had never ventured **(7)** ..... the outskirts of their towns and villages. The railway brought them **(8)** ..... freedom and enlightenment.

   In the 19th century, the railway in Britain **(9)** ..... something more than just the business of carrying goods and passengers. Trains were associated with romance, adventure and, frequently, **(10)** ..... luxury. The great steam locomotives that thundered across the land were the jet airliners of their **(11)** ..... , carrying passengers in comfort over vast distances in unimaginably short times. But the railways **(12)** ..... more than revolutionise travel; they also **(13)** ..... a distinctive and permanent mark on the British landscape. Whole towns and industrial centres **(14)** ..... up around major rail junctions, monumental bridges and viaducts crossed rivers and valleys and the railway stations themselves became **(15)** ..... places to spend time between journeys.

0	**A**	amount	**B**	figure	**C**	sum	**D**	quantity
1	**A**	revolve	**B**	enclose	**C**	encircle	**D**	orbit
2	**A**	altering	**B**	amending	**C**	adapting	**D**	adjusting
3	**A**	route	**B**	way	**C**	line	**D**	course
4	**A**	pursued	**B**	followed	**C**	succeeded	**D**	chased
5	**A**	cancelling	**B**	subtracting	**C**	cutting	**D**	abolishing
6	**A**	reach	**B**	capacity	**C**	facility	**D**	hold
7	**A**	further	**B**	over	**C**	beyond	**D**	above
8	**A**	larger	**B**	higher	**C**	bigger	**D**	greater
9	**A**	served	**B**	functioned	**C**	represented	**D**	performed
10	**A**	considerable	**B**	generous	**C**	plentiful	**D**	sizeable
11	**A**	date	**B**	stage	**C**	day	**D**	phase
12	**A**	caused	**B**	did	**C**	produced	**D**	turned
13	**A**	laid	**B**	set	**C**	settled	**D**	left
14	**A**	jumped	**B**	stood	**C**	burst	**D**	sprang
15	**A**	preferable	**B**	liked	**C**	desirable	**D**	wanted

(Item 0: **B** figure is circled)

Part 2

For questions **16–30**, complete the following article by writing each missing word in the correct box on your answer sheet. **Use only one word for each space.** The exercise begins with an example **(0)**.

Example: | 0 | to | 0 |

Enjoy the benefits of stress!

Are you looking forward to another busy week? You should be according **(0)** ..... some experts. They argue that the stress encountered in **(16)** ..... daily lives is not only good for us, but essential to survival. They say that the response to stress, which creates a chemical called adrenalin, helps the mind and body to act quickly **(17)** ..... emergencies. Animals and human beings use it to meet the hostile conditions **(18)** ..... exist on the planet.

Whilst nobody denies the pressures of everyday life, what is surprising is that we are yet to develop successful ways of dealing with them. **(19)** ..... the experts consider the current strategies to **(20)** ..... inadequate and often dangerous. They believe that **(21)** ..... of trying to manage our response to stress with drugs or relaxation techniques, we must exploit it. Apparently, research shows that people **(22)** ..... create conditions of stress for **(23)** ..... by doing exciting and risky sports or looking for challenges, cope much better with life's problems. Activities of this type **(24)** ..... been shown to create a lot of emotion; people may actually cry or feel extremely uncomfortable. But there is a point **(25)** ..... which they realise they have succeeded and know that it was a positive experience. This is because we learn through challenge and difficulty. That's **(26)** ..... we get our wisdom. Few of **(27)** ..... , unfortunately, understand **(28)** ..... fact. For example, many people believe they suffer from stress at work, and take time off **(29)** ..... a result. Yet it has been found in some companies that by far **(30)** ..... healthiest people are those with the most responsibility. So next time you're in a stressful situation, just remember that it will be a positive learning experience and could also benefit your health!

Part 3

In **most** lines of the following text, there is **either** a spelling **or** a punctuation error. For each numbered line **31–46**, write the correctly spelt word or show the correct punctuation in the box on your answer sheet. **Some lines are correct.** Indicate these lines with a tick (✓) in the box. The exercise begins with three examples (**0**), (**00**) and (**000**).

Examples:

0	*chicken, fish*	0
00	*restaurant*	00
000	✓	000

Ice cream

0	Spaghetti with chicken fish and chips, Indian tea. No, these are not
00	items on a restrant menu, but ice cream flavours sold in a shop high
000	in the Venezuelan Andes. At this particular ice cream shop, you are
31	presented with a choice of 683 vareities. It is no surprise, therefore,
32	that it is listed in many referance books as the place which has the
33	most flavours in the world. 'I wanted to do something different, the
34	owner said, 'so I bougth an ice cream machine. It's the best investment
35	I've ever made.' The portuguese businessman started experimenting
36	17 years ago, trying to make avocado ice cream. He finally found a
37	sucessful formula and became addicted to experimenting. Soon his
38	imagination knew no limits. Whatever food you think of his shop has
39	the ice cream version. 'When I'm looking a long the rows of food in a
40	supermarket, I imediately ask myself which flavour I could use next,' the
41	owner said. This can occasionally leed to problems. He once made
42	an ice cream with a chilli flavour that was so strong his customer's
43	complained that their mouths were burning. The owner, Mr. Olvero
44	who keeps the ice cream recipes in his head, says that there is still
45	room for more flavours. He adds that he would be grateful for any
46	suggestions for the shop that he plans to open in the near future

Part 4

For questions **47–61**, read the texts on pages **24** and **25**. Use the words in the box to the right of the texts to form **one** word that fits in the same numbered space in the texts. Write the new word in the correct box on your answer sheet. The exercise begins with an example (**0**).

Example:

0	historic	0

LEAFLET

The museum of advertising and packaging

In the heart of the **(0)** ..... city of Gloucester, visitors can experience a sentimental journey back through the memories of their childhood, all brought vividly to life again at the Museum of Advertising and Packaging. The result of one man's **(47)** ..... , the museum is the **(48)** ..... of twenty-five years' research and collecting by Robert Opie. This **(49)** ..... remarkable collection, the largest of its type in the world, now numbers some 300,000 items relating to the **(50)** ..... of our consumer society. The **(51)** ..... of packets, tins, bottles and signs shows the variety which was introduced into the shops. For this reason, the colourful exhibition is called a *Century of Shopping History*. The change in shopping habits is in part attributable to the development of the **(52)** ..... power of advertising, together with **(53)** ..... advanced technology.

---

(0)	HISTORY
(47)	ENTHUSE
(48)	PRODUCE
(49)	TRUE
(50)	EVOLVE
(51)	INCLUDE
(52)	PERSUADE
(53)	INCREASE

ENCYCLOPAEDIA ENTRY

Making paper

It is **(54)** ..... believed that paper was invented in China. A **(55)** ..... Chinese court official by the name of Ts'ai Lun first developed a material that was **(56)** ..... similar to the paper that we use today. The **(57)** ..... details of the story are unknown, but it is thought that among his ingredients were bits of tree bark, old rags and fishing nets. Ts'ai Lun's inspiration came **(58)** ..... from making observations of insects that construct a thin-shelled nest from tiny pieces of wood fibre. The first industrial machine for making paper in a continuous roll was perfected in France in 1799. Since then, the world has had an **(59)** ..... supply of paper. Today paper **(60)** ..... can offer a wide variety of paper types, from fine white paper to tough brown **(61)** ..... paper. These days, paper-making is no longer such a time-consuming activity.

(54) TRADITION

(55) RESOURCE

(56) APPEAR

(57) FACT

(58) PRIME

(59) INTERRUPT

(60) MANUFACTURE

(61) WRAP

Part 5

For questions **62–74**, read the following film review and use the information in it to complete the letter to a friend who has asked you about the film. Write the new words in the correct boxes **on your answer sheet**. The words you need **do not occur** in the film review. **Use no more than two words for each gap.** The exercise begins with an example (**0**).

Example:

0	anything positive	0

FILM REVIEW

Fun Time is a recently released film that has received an enormous amount of publicity all over the world, but I find it very hard to think of a complimentary remark to make about it. The plot is definitely not clear and simple, and the majority of people will find it unintelligible. In my opinion, the director, James Carson, is very much overrated. The truth is that he ignores the basic principles of film-making and overuses special effects. All the characters lack credibility and the audience I sat with started to become restless after about thirty minutes. Because of this, a lot of people will not stay until the end. They will vote with their feet. In addition, the actors are playing characters which are quite inappropriate for them; the soundtrack is absolutely deafening, and the inadequate lighting makes some scenes almost invisible. What is more, the general style of the film is derived from earlier and better films. It completely lacks originality and it looks amateurish. Even if you are a real fan of James Carson's films, this one will try your patience. It's certainly not a film I'd bother going to a second time.

LETTER

You asked me about Fun Time. I haven't seen it, but I've read a review. The critic said he couldn't think of (0) ..... to say about it. He thought the story was far (62) ..... and that most people won't be able to (63) ..... it. It is his opinion that the director has a better reputation than (64) ..... . In particular, he thinks that special effects are used (65) ..... . Also the characters were impossible to (66) ..... and that, because the film started to become (67) ..... after only half an hour, many people will probably (68) ..... of the cinema before the end. His view is that the actors are playing the (69) ..... and that the music is much (70) ..... . Some scenes can hardly (71) ..... at all because of the poor lighting. He didn't think the film had any (72) ..... at all and to him it didn't look at all (73) ..... . His conclusion is that even those who are (74) ..... James Carson's films will find this one hard work. I think I'll be giving it a miss and I suggest you do the same.

Part 6

For questions **75–80**, read the following text and then choose from the list **A–I** given below the best phrase to fill each of the spaces. Indicate your answers on the separate answer sheet. Each correct phrase may only be used once. **Some of the suggested answers do not fit at all.**

The problems of public speaking

For most people, one of the biggest fears in life is having to make a speech, whether at school, at a wedding, or in our business lives. There are several good reasons for this, not least amongst them the fear that no-one will have the slightest interest in what you are saying. If you are on stage, as is often the case with such speeches, there's no problem. **(75)** ..... you to see the audience, because the lights blind you the moment you step up. The only area of the stage that may have no light whatsoever is the lectern where you put your notes – it will be in total darkness.

(76) ..... you probably realise that you've left your glasses at home. **(77)** ..... , you now have to improvise a 40-minute speech based on those few words of your notes you can actually see. It's then that the technical faults start to come into play. First, if you need any, your slides and illustrations won't work. **(78)** ..... , you'll accidentally push the wrong button and show everything upside down. **(79)** ..... , they will show the wrong picture at the wrong time, and even jump a couple. If you're lucky, the lights will fail at this point and the speech will have to be abandoned!

(80) ..... the technical support is excellent, which allows you to make a good and lasting impression. It's important to start well. To fight nerves, it's a good idea to grip the lectern with both hands, but not too tightly, because they have been known to collapse!

A   It's at about this time that
B   If professionals are in charge
C   It's always a good thing
D   If it's in your hands
E   Fortunately, it is not possible for
F   There are times, however, when
G   However, if it isn't the case
H   Despite having spent ages preparing it
I   With this in mind

PAPER 4   LISTENING (approximately 45 minutes)

Part 1

You will hear part of a lecture in which a man called Tom Trueman talks about golf courses and the environment. For questions **1–8**, complete the sentences.

You will hear the recording twice.

The recent popularity of golf resulted from local success in

	1

A demand for new golf courses attracted the interest of both

| | **2** | and businessmen.
|---|---|

Many developers made the mistake of building golf courses to

| | **3** | standards.
|---|---|

Golf courses tend to be used by people who live in

	4

Some people think that golf courses look too much like

	5

Trees planted on golf courses are often chosen because they

	6

Tom suggests that golf courses could be

| | **7** | as well.
|---|---|

Tom would like to see golf courses integrated into both the

| | **8** | and the ecology.
|---|---|

Part 2

You will hear a radio talk given by a photographer. For questions **9–16**, complete the sentences.

Listen very carefully as you will hear the recording ONCE only.

General Information

Ian says that people prefer to take photographs of

| | **9** | things.

Ian suggests that photograph albums have replaced people's

| | **10**

He says that you should use | | **11**

in order to take good pictures.

Ian recommends that you should | | **12** poor photographs.

Landscapes

Ian suggests taking pictures from different | | **13**

He suggests including a varying amount of

| | **14** in the picture.

Portraits

Ian recommends checking all the | | **15** first.

He recommends photographing children at their own | | **16**

Part 3

You will hear an interview on a train with two friends, Jane and Chris, chefs who both won prizes in the National Railway Chef of the Year competition. For questions **17–24**, choose the correct answer **A**, **B**, **C** or **D**.

You will hear the recording twice.

17 What was Chris's attitude to the competition?

    A   He was worried about the quality of his dishes.
    B   He was afraid time might be a bit of a problem.
    C   He admitted he'd been looking forward to the challenge.
    D   He said conditions were similar to his normal routine.

18 Jane admitted that the greatest problem she faced during the competition was having to

    A   work in a very small space.
    B   be original when travelling at speed.
    C   prepare a meal so quickly.
    D   create a meal with so little money.

19 What do both Chris and Jane feel is unique about their job?

    A   the close contact with the customers
    B   the necessity to do everything at the same time
    C   the opportunity to be creative
    D   the need to be focused on the job

20 What do Chris and Jane feel about what they cook on board the train?

    A   They approve of the menus created for them.
    B   They consider themselves more adventurous than other chefs.
    C   They would like to have more freedom of choice.
    D   They are happy to adapt their ideas to suit the job.

21 Chris thought being a railway chef would suit him mainly because it would enable him to

    A   show his ability to work under pressure.
    B   use the skills he had been trained for.
    C   do something out of the ordinary.
    D   satisfy his love of travelling.

22 What is often Jane's initial reaction when things spill over?

    A She asks another member of staff to help her clear up.
    B She blames the train driver for the accident.
    C She tells herself to keep a closer watch next time.
    D She says nasty things to the other staff.

23 What does Chris say caused his worst disaster?

    A leaving things to burn under the grill
    B dropping the main course on the floor
    C losing his concentration when cooking
    D not keeping an eye on the oven temperature

24 How does Jane react to Chris's suggestion for the future?

    A She's determined that she'll join him if she can.
    B She's looking forward to a challenge of that kind.
    C She's afraid Chris wouldn't want her company.
    D She'd be unable to take part in that kind of activity.

Part 4

You will hear five short extracts in which different people are talking about works of art they would buy if they had £20,000.

You will hear the recording twice. While you listen you must complete both tasks.

TASK ONE

For questions **25–29**, match the extracts as you hear them with the works of art the people would buy, listed **A–H**.

A   works of a more subtle nature

B   works which make a statement

C   well-known works from different artists

D   works from the past

E   copies of works by famous people

F   works portraying scenes from nature

G   works recently on show

H   works from artists just starting out

	25
	26
	27
	28
	29

TASK TWO

For questions **30–34**, match the extracts as you hear them with the comment each speaker makes about the world of art, listed **A–H**.

A   Artists should try their best to be commercially successful.

B   Art should be something you would never want to part with.

C   Artists should not try to alter their style to suit the market.

D   To make money out of art, you should be able to spot a bargain.

E   Artists should be appreciated more during their lifetime.

F   People should be wary of buying imitations.

G   Art should always be bought on impulse.

H   Art should not be regarded as an investment.

	30
	31
	32
	33
	34

PAPER 5   SPEAKING (15 minutes)

There are two examiners. One (the interlocutor) conducts the test, providing you with the necessary materials and explaining what you have to do. The other examiner (the assessor) is introduced to you, but then takes no further part in the interaction.

Part 1 (3 minutes)

The interlocutor first asks you and your partner a few questions. You are then asked to find out some information about each other, on topics such as hobbies, interests, future plans, etc. You are then asked further questions by the interlocutor.

Part 2 (4 minutes)

You are each given the opportunity to talk for about a minute, and to comment briefly after your partner has spoken.

   The interlocutor gives you a set of pictures and asks you to talk about them for about one minute. It is important to listen carefully to the interlocutor's instructions. The interlocutor then asks your partner a question about your pictures and your partner responds briefly.

   You are then given another set of pictures to look at. Your partner talks about these pictures for about one minute. This time the interlocutor asks you a question about your partner's pictures and you respond briefly.

Part 3 (approximately 4 minutes)

In this part of the test you and your partner are asked to talk together. The interlocutor places a new set of pictures on the table between you. This stimulus provides the basis for a discussion. The interlocutor explains what you have to do.

Part 4 (approximately 4 minutes)

The interlocutor asks some further questions, which leads to a more general discussion of what you have talked about in Part 3. You may comment on your partner's answers if you wish.

Test 2

PAPER 1 READING (1 hour 15 minutes)

Part 1

Answer questions **1–16** by referring to the magazine article on page **37**, in which four naturalists explain their choice of most inspiring book about the environment. Indicate your answers **on the separate answer sheet**.

For questions **1–16**, answer by choosing from the four naturalists (**A–D**) on page 37. Some of the choices may be required more than once.

Which naturalist

says that the book contained a wider range of material than other books he/she owned?	1..........
says that the human race is often blamed for its destructive relationship with wildlife?	2..........
says that the book can make the organisation of a particular animal group clear to an observer?	3..........
praises the author's desire to make the work accessible to the non-specialist?	4..........
explains what motivated him/her to start drawing?	5..........
describes experiencing a change of mood when reading the book?	6..........
praises the book for both its use of language and depth of feeling?	7..........
describes the sensory experiences evoked by the book?	8..........
thinks the book encouraged greater optimism about a personal skill?	9..........
mentions an initial reluctance to become involved in investigating environmental issues?	10..........
attributes the skill of the illustrator to extensive observation?	11..........
has come into contact with many leading environmental figures through work?	12..........
attributes the immediate appeal of the book to its illustrations?	13..........
first read the book at a time when experiencing problems?	14..........
comments on the illustrator's ability to show animal behaviour through deceptively simple pictures?	15..........
says that no other book has proved to be as good as the one nominated?	16..........

Natural Books

We invited four leading naturalists to tell us about the wildlife classic that has influenced them most

A
Geoffrey Lean

At least it wasn't hard to choose the author. As an environmental journalist, one advantage of longevity is that I have had the chance to meet some of the giants who pioneered thinking in the field. Of these, none stood, indeed, still stands, taller than a small, frail woman, Barbara Ward. I can't think of anyone else more at the heart of environmental issues in post-war Europe. She has synthesised her experience of various environmental movements into her own compelling philosophy. Unwillingly 'volunteered' to cover the field, I found, as a young journalist, that she, more than anyone, made it all make sense.

Picking the book was much harder. It could have been *Only One Earth* or *Progress for a Small Planet*. But despite its title (which sounded old-fashioned, even in 1976), *The Home of Man* is, to me, Barbara's most important book. Its focus is on the explosive growth of the world's cities, but its canvas is the great themes to which she devoted her life. It is as eloquent and as impassioned a plea as exists for what we would now call 'sustainable human development'. In the hundreds of books I have read since, I have yet to meet its equal.

B
Linda Bennett

When I open the pages of *Signals for Survival* by Niko Tinbergen, I can hear the long calls of herring gulls, recall the smell of the guano in the hot sun and visualise the general hullabaloo of the colony. This book explains superbly, through words and pictures, the fascinating world of animal communication.

Read *Signals for Survival* and then watch any gull colony, and the frenzy of activity changes from apparent chaos to a highly efficient social structure. You can see which birds are partners, where the boundaries are and, later on in the season, whole families can be recognised.

A distinguished behaviourist, Niko Tinbergen came from that rare breed of academics who wish to explain their findings to the layperson. His collaboration in this book with one of this century's most talented wildlife artists, Eric Ennion, was inspirational and has produced a book of interest to anyone with a love of wildlife. His spontaneous style of painting came from years of watching and understanding birds. With just a minimal amount of line and colour, he brings to life how one gull is an aggressor, how another shows appeasement. This is the art of a true field naturalist.

C
Lee Durrell

Most definitely, *My Family and Other Animals* by Gerald Durrell is the book that has had the greatest influence on my life. Beyond the obvious reason that it ultimately led me to a wonderful husband, and an exciting career in conservation, this extraordinary book once and for all defined my devotion to the natural world.

I was doing research work into animal vocalisations in Madagascar when I first read the book. I had been there two years and was discouraged by the number of setbacks I was encountering but when, at the end of the day, I opened *My Family and Other Animals* to where I had left off the night before, the world became a brighter place. Animals, people, joy and beauty inextricably woven together – a microcosm of a world worth saving.

Many people say that our species is the worst because of the terrible things we have done to the others. But I like to think back to Gerald as a boy in *My Family and Other Animals*, looking at the world's inhabitants as a whole, a family whose members, be they good, bad or indifferent, are nevertheless so intertwined as to be inseparable. And that is a concept we all need to grasp.

D
Bruce Pearson

A copy of *The Shell Bird Book*, by James Fisher, found its way into my school library shortly after it was first published in 1966. I was drawn to it at once, especially to the 48 colour plates of birds by Eric Ennion, painted, as the jacket puts it, ... with particular skill and charm'. It was those Ennion images which captured my attention.

I already had copies of other bird books and had spent several holidays learning to identify birds. They encouraged me to begin sketching what I saw as an aid to identification. But in *The Shell Bird Book* there was so much more to feast on. As well as the glorious Ennion paintings, there were chapters on migrants and migration, a review of the history of birds in Britain, and, best of all, a chapter on birds in music, literature and art.

It was the broad span of ornithological information and the exciting images that steered me towards being more of a generalist in my appreciation of birds and the natural world. The book made it clear that my emotional and creative response to nature was as valid and as possible as a rational and scientific one. And, as art was a stronger subject for me than maths or physics, I began to see a door opening for me.

Part 2

For questions **17–22**, choose which of the paragraphs **A–G** on page **39** fit into the numbered gaps in the following newspaper article. There is one extra paragraph which does not fit in any of the gaps. Indicate your answers **on the separate answer sheet**.

In search of true north – and the man behind Halley's comet

Dr Toby Clark, a researcher at the British Geological Survey, aims to retrace Sir Edmund Halley's quest to chart compass variations. Anjana Ahuja reports.

Astronomer Sir Edmund Halley (1656–1742) is best known for the comet that bears his name. Yet one of his greatest accomplishments, in the eyes of his contemporaries, was to chart, using calculations made on his sea voyages on the warship *Paramore*, the 'variations of the compass'. These variations are now known as 'declination', that is, the angle between magnetic north and true geographical north. Without it, sailors were unable to correct their compasses. It was therefore impossible to deduce longitude precisely and navigate the oceans.

17

This voyage took him and his crew to Rio de Janeiro, down past South Georgia, up again to Newfoundland and back to England. From these travels Halley published, in 1701, a '*New and Correct Chart shewing the Variations of the Compasse in the Western and Southern Oceans*'. More sophisticated successors to this primitive cartographic effort proved indispensable to seamen for more than a century, before a slow change in the terrestrial magnetic field rendered them inaccurate.

18

£70,000 will have to be raised before he embarks, and Sir Vivian Fuchs, who led the first cross-Antarctica expedition, is providing support for his efforts to do this.

Dr Clark became fascinated by Halley during a two-year posting to Halley Station in Antarctica, where he read biographies of the great scientist.

19

It was during this period that Halley developed a diving bell and also advised Sir Isaac Newton during his writing of *Principia Mathematica*, the foundation of classical physics. Recreating the voyage, Dr Clark says, will afford Halley the recognition he deserves. The projected expedition, which he has entitled 'In the Wake of the *Paramore*', will also have scientific merit.

20

The data collected should help to refine the existing mathematical model of Earth's magnetic field, called the international geomagnetic reference field. 'It is common to measure the size but not the direction of the magnetic field. That's because you need to know true north to measure the direction,' says Dr Clark.

21

Dr Clark hopes that his measurements will plug any gaps in its coverage of the Atlantic Ocean and, he points out, it is also useful to have ground-based measurements as a comparison. It is easy to forget just how significant Halley's Atlantic journey really was. It was the first dedicated scientific expedition on the seas and

Halley became the first civilian who was appointed naval captain to pursue what many regarded as an obsession with declination. Does Dr Clark possess the credentials to make his parallel voyage a success?

22	

And does he share Halley's obsessive trait? 'I am prepared to give up my life for eight months to do this, so I suppose some people might think I'm obsessed. But I wouldn't want to sail across the Atlantic again without a good reason. Halley, and his fascinating life, have given me a real sense of purpose.'

A 'On our expedition we can use global positioning satellites to determine that.' The British Geological Survey and the United States Navy have offered to supply instruments. By chance, a Danish satellite will be taking similar measurements over the globe.

B If all goes well, Halley's accomplishments will be celebrated once again. Dr Clark, himself a keen sailor, plans to commemorate the three-hundredth anniversary of Halley's trip by retracing the route of the *Paramore*.

C As well as spending two years in Antarctica and working in the geomagnetic group at the British Geological Survey, he has already sailed the 13,000 kilometres from Rio de Janeiro to England. He envisages that the expedition will be completed in four stages, with four different crews.

D So it was that Halley, one of only two men in the land at that time paid to conduct scientific research, set sail for the Cape Verde Islands with the grand plan of charting declination in the North and South Atlantic. The trip was quickly aborted because of crew insubordination, but Halley returned to the seas a second time.

E It will involve making the measurements that Halley made, but with far more precise instruments. These measurements need to be updated because the terrestrial magnetic field is slowly but constantly changing.

F In addition, the charts that he produced are celebrated by cartographers – they are said to be the first maps that used lines to delineate physical quantities. The contours became known briefly as 'halleyan' lines.

G 'Halley led a remarkable life,' Dr Clark says. 'He was not only a respected scientist but also led expeditions. He was not just an astronomer but also did research in geophysics. While he was Astronomer Royal, he mapped the positions of the stars, and also found time for other interests.'

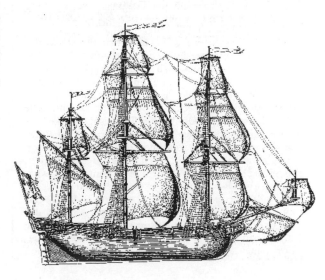

Part 3

Read the following newspaper article and answer questions **23–28** on page **41**. **On your answer sheet**, indicate the letter **A**, **B**, **C** or **D** against the number of each question, **23–28**. Give only one answer to each question.

The Tartan Museum

The modern, cheese-wedge buildings of Scotland's national museum contrast sharply with its historic Edinburgh location. But would its contents be as striking? Sally Varlow went to visit the museum just before it opened

You cannot miss it. At first it was only the outside of the new Museum of Scotland that was unmissable, stuck on the corner of Chambers Street in Edinburgh, with its huge, yellow sandstone tower and cheese-wedge buildings, topped by a hulk of a hanging garden. Last winter the building was greeted with a mix of modernist architectural applause ('masterpiece', 'stunning'), cautious approval ('striking') and outright hostility. This winter, now that the inside is almost ready for the opening, the exhibitions themselves look set for a similar fate.

Forget the does-it-tell-a-nation's-story, is-it-chronological debate. The answers are definitely yes; it is a many-splendoured dream-coat of stories, each hung about a precious historic object, and there is an outline timescale that helps visitors get their bearings but does not strait-jacket the displays. And no, it does not let its lovely national treasures – such as Mary Queen of Scots' jewels and the Holyrood chapel silver – get swamped in national pride.

The real issue here, assuming that the collections are properly preserved, is whether people will find the museum interesting enough to come back. Dr David Clarke, the head of exhibitions, insists that a visit should be a pleasurable, visual experience, and that it is designed not for specialists but for those with little prior knowledge. Despite this liberalism, Clarke is a convincing purist when it comes to what is on show. Mock-ups and scenes from the past that rely heavily on imagination are out. For Clarke, they are tantamount to 'giving a complete statement of certainty about what the past was like, which', he explains, 'would be wrong. The public deserves the truth.' The result is that, at this museum, what you see is what the experts know. But the question for today's visitor is whether the objects' stories can be told vividly enough merely with explanation panels, captions and multi-media interpretation

and using barely 30 computers in total around the museum.

Less than three days before the opening, it is still difficult to be sure. Some impressions are clear, though, and it is not just the panoramic views of Edinburgh Castle that take your breath away. Step inside and what immediately hits you is the sequence of spaces. Galleries open one into another, different sizes, different shapes, all with pale walls that are wood-panelled to look like large blocks of stone and inset with deep display cases. Shafts of daylight stream through arrow-slit windows and cascade down from the roof lights. There is room to ponder and enjoy every item on display.

Thanks to the 12-member Junior board, set up three years ago with 9- to 12-year-olds drawn from all over Scotland, the museum also has a Discovery Centre. What the group really wanted was to be able to ride through the displays, Dr Clarke admits. They lost that one, but won a dedicated children's hands-on centre in what should have been the temporary exhibition gallery. As a result, the Twentieth Century gallery, on the top floor, is the only temporary exhibition. Due to change after three years, it is a hotchpotch of objects chosen by Scottish people and other personalities as the items that have had most impact on life in Scotland in the twentieth century. The Prime Minister's suggestion was an electric guitar. Others went for televisions, Thermos flasks and favourite toys. Although the idea is fun, somehow it feels like a lightweight solution that has floated up to the top of the building, not a proper attempt to address serious issues. It may seem less frothy when the computerised bank of personal reasons and recollections goes live next week.

Overall, Dr Clarke seems right when he suggests that 'objects open windows on the past more vividly than anything else'. As for the modernist architecture: it works brilliantly from the inside and the top, but whether it is in the right location is another matter.

23 How does the writer expect people to react to the exhibitions?

    A   They will be more interested in the buildings than the exhibitions.
    B   There will be a predominance of negative feelings.
    C   Their expectations are too high to be satisfied.
    D   There will be no consensus of opinion.

24 What does the writer say about the historical focus of the exhibitions?

    A   The adherence to a strict historical timescale is the most important aspect.
    B   The historical background of a period is characterised through particular objects.
    C   The displays are not always easy to place in a historical context.
    D   The importance of national treasures in a historical context is exaggerated.

25 How does Dr Clarke feel about the historical displays?

    A   There should be something for everyone with an interest in Scottish history.
    B   They should stimulate the visitors' own imaginations.
    C   They should show only what is factually accurate.
    D   They should recreate history in as realistic a way as possible.

26 What is the most impressive aspect of the inside of the museum, according to the writer?

    A   the design
    B   the lighting
    C   the items on display
    D   the number of galleries

27 What does the writer think of the temporary exhibition?

    A   It deserves a better location in the museum.
    B   Its realisation does not satisfy the original concept.
    C   Its contents should be more accessible to children.
    D   It is difficult to understand the rationale for it.

28 What is the writer's overall impression of the museum?

    A   She thinks it provides inadequate coverage of Scotland's historic past.
    B   She finds its approach insufficiently different from that of any other museum.
    C   She considers the building to be impractical for its purpose.
    D   She feels unsure as to whether the exhibitions will live up to their setting.

Part 4

Answer questions **29–47** by referring to the interviews with talented people on pages **43–44**. Indicate your answers **on the separate answer sheet**.

For questions **29–47**, answer by choosing from the sections of the article (**A–E**). Some of the choices may be required more than once.

Which person

— says he is keen to avoid producing uninspired work? **29**..........

— admits to making technical errors in his work that he is unlikely to repeat? **30**..........

— disagrees with a commonly held view about the kind of work he does? **31**..........

— surprised the interviewer by his lack of relevant experience at the start of his career? **32**..........

— had been trying for a long time to achieve recognition? **33**..........

— admits that he is no longer motivated by the same things as when he was younger? **34**..........

— continued with his education after becoming disillusioned with the work he was doing? **35**..........

— mentions the respect he has for a fellow performer? **36**..........

— is uncertain about the funding he will get for his current work? **37**..........

— says he only became committed to his work when he recognised his own talents? **38**..........

— was about to abandon his career ambitions at one point? **39**..........

— is praised by the interviewer for risking a change of direction in his work? **40**..........

— describes how he would be satisfied with a low level of commercial success? **41**..........

— describes the benefits of a particular working relationship? **42**..........

— talks about the difficulties he might encounter with a new form of work? **43**..........

— became well-known as a result of a television appearance? **44**..........

— describes how he felt when he started to work with others who shared his views? **45**..........

— is optimistic that his recent success will make up for past disappointments? **46**..........

— has a career history that prompts the interviewer to say his success was inevitable? **47**..........

Fame and Fortune

Imogen Edwards-Jones interviews some of the new British talent, from poet to pop star, heading for the top

A

Nick Grosso, in his early 30s, is the author of three critically acclaimed plays. He is currently adapting his first play, *Peaches*, into a screenplay. 'It's low budget, but we don't know how low,' he explains. 'It certainly won't be over £30 million, but then it could be 30 quid.'

Although obviously gifted, the most extraordinary thing about Nick is that before he wrote *Peaches* he had never been to or read a play in his life. 'When I wrote the play, I never even imagined it would get put on,' he says. 'It's set in a car. I probably wouldn't do that now because I know the logistical problems. I knew absolutely nothing then.'

He left school at 16, only to return a year later. After A-levels, he enrolled at the Young People's Theatre. 'I realised I wanted to write for actors. I wanted my writing to be heard rather than read because of the rhythm and rhyme,' he says. 'Suddenly I was surrounded by like-minded people. It was the first time I'd been in an educational environment and actually enjoyed myself. It was very stimulating.'

B

Comedian **Simon Pegg**, 28, has come a long way in his career since studying drama at Bristol University. He is currently writing a television comedy series, and has just finished a punishing tour around the country with comedy star Steve Coogan.

He's always worked hard. Even as far back as Bristol, he was honing his art in comedy clubs. 'It was very theoretical at university,' remembers Simon. 'It made me realise I didn't want to be a straight actor and that I'd always been more interested in comedy. People think that comedy is the hardest job in the world and it really isn't. If you've got the courage and you've got good material, it's a wonderful thing to make people laugh.'

He has performed with the comic team Funny Business, but it is his relationship with Steve Coogan that has proved the most fruitful. 'He saw my show and, as I was a huge fan of his, he could probably see me mimicking him,' admits Simon. 'It was terrifying the first time I met him but we've become good mates. We have a great rapport. We make each other laugh and it's a really creative atmosphere.'

C

Ciaran McMenamin, 24, came to the public's attention when he disco-danced into their living rooms as the lead in the series *The Young Person's Guide To Becoming A Rock Star*. The critical reaction was extremely positive and his subsequent rise has been meteoric. 'It's been a really good showcase for me,' he says with a smile. 'I'm now in a situation where I can pick and choose what I do, which is what I've always wanted.' It is an unusually comfortable position to be in, especially when you consider that he has only just graduated. But glance at Ciaran's early career, and it's obvious such recognition was always on the cards.

Encouraged by his mother, he went from playing lead roles at school to the Ulster Youth Theatre, where he stayed for four years. 'Basically I was using acting as an excuse not to do homework,' laughs Ciaran. 'But I suddenly decided I wanted to make a go of it because I had a knack for it, and a passion for it.'

Now he is more or less sitting back and waiting for the plaudits to roll in – but ask him what he thinks of the fame game and he suddenly becomes pensive. 'When you're 18, you think you'll love the photos and the interviews but you soon realise it's not what you're acting for. It's not about that. It's about getting respect for doing good work.'

D

Neil Taylor, 25, is the lead singer in the pop band Matrix, which has just signed a three-album deal with Domino Records. Neil and the other half of Matrix, Rick Brown, are already tipped to be huge when their single, *Chimera*, is released shortly. 'The record company's idea of good sales is very different to mine,' he says. 'They're talking smash hit, but I've no idea. For me, if two people buy it, I'll be happy.'

Unlike so many new pop sensations, Neil has actually worked very hard for his success. He left school at 16 and has been trying to break into the music business ever since. 'It's funny how things happen,' he says. 'I'd been slogging away doing student gigs for eight years and I was starting to get a bit jaded. I was just about to give up when this happened.' By 'this' he means meeting Rick Brown, who already had contacts at Domino, and forming Matrix. It couldn't have happened at a better time. 'There were times when I was thoroughly depressed – and I've been in some atrocious bands. But hopefully it will all have been worth it.'

E

Poet and author **Stephen Richards** is 27 years old and has won more prizes, awards and academic honours than anyone twice his age. He is already well known on the poetry circuit, where he has been touring and giving several readings a week for the past six years. Now his first novel, *Hidden*, will be published in March. 'It's a story of obsessive love. It was a very strong idea that I couldn't do as a poem.'

Stephen was a huge fan of creative writing at school, but became disenchanted with education later on. 'I decided not to go to university but it wasn't until I became very bored with stuffing envelopes at a theatre that I decided I should.' After university, he published his first work, a children's book, in 1992. 'I don't think my parents expected me to be a writer – they always thought I'd be a reader because that's all I did as a child.' With his poetry receiving such critical acclaim, his move into novels is indeed brave. 'There's a framework with my poetry and less scope for me to do something hideously wrong,' he explains. 'Because a novel can be any length of words, there are more words that could be bad words. My main ambition is not to get into a pattern where I'm just churning stuff out without worrying about the quality.'

PAPER 2   WRITING (2 hours)

Part 1

1   You recently took part in an exchange programme in Canada where you stayed with a Canadian student for four weeks. The editor of the English language newspaper at your college has now asked you to write an article for the newspaper, describing what you enjoyed about your visit, explaining any problems you had and encouraging readers to take part in the exchange programme.

Read the extracts from the letters from the editor of the newspaper and from the Canadian student below and, on page **46**, the original advertisement for the exchange programme, on which you have made notes. Then, **using the information appropriately**, write the article, describing what you enjoyed about the exchange programme, outlining any problems you had and persuading more people to take part.

… and so, can you write an article for the paper telling us about your visit? It sounded great! Don't forget to tell us about the problems as well as all the good bits. I'd like your article to persuade more people to do an exchange because it's so good for their English. I hope they'll read your article and seriously consider taking part.
Thanks ….

… We had such a great time, didn't we? I'm really glad you enjoyed it. It's always a bit scary going somewhere new but I hope we made you feel at home. I know you were a bit worried about your English but you were great. Just think – you spoke nothing but English for 4 weeks! It must have been tiring!

I'm sorry we didn't have time to show you the sights a bit more but the camping trip was good, wasn't it? Mum wants me to apologise again for the fact that you had to share a room with me but it was the only way we could manage it.

I'm really looking forward to visiting you next year.

STUDENT EXCHANGE PROGRAMME

IMPROVE YOUR ENGLISH AND <u>MAKE A FRIEND</u>!

true

We offer exchange programmes in Canada, USA and Britain. Choose to stay for <u>4</u> – 8 weeks.

best

really kind – food very good

We find the families and then match you up with somebody your own age so you can share their <u>social life</u>. All our <u>host families</u> will show you the <u>local area</u> and include you as a member of the family. In return, you agree to host the foreign student in your family the next year.

not much to do in the evenings, but...

Rocky Mountains – bears! great camping

more than I thought

You need to pay your <u>travel costs</u> and bring <u>pocket money</u> and we do the rest.

didn't take enough!

Phone today for more information – 0208 456 8475.

Now write your **article** as outlined on page **45** (approximately 250 words). You should use your own words as far as possible.

Part 2

Choose **one** of the following writing tasks. Your answer should follow exactly the instructions given. Write approximately 250 words.

2   There is going to be an international music festival in your area. You have seen the following notice in the local newspaper.

International Music Festival – Judges Wanted

Can you help? Thousands of groups and musicians have applied to play in our 3-day festival. We need judges to help us decide which groups and musicians to accept. If you are interested in working with us, please write explaining:

- which types of music you think we should have
- what your own tastes in music are
- what would make you a good judge.

Write your **letter of application**.

3   It has become very popular for students to work in another country during their vacation. You have been asked to write the entry on **your** country to be included in a new book called *A Guide to Temporary Jobs Around the World*, covering the following points:
- types of holiday jobs available and how to find them
- pay and conditions
- advice about possible problems students may face when working in your country.

You should write about 2 or 3 vacation jobs.

Write your **contribution** for the guidebook.

4   You are a member of the students' committee at a college where there are many students from all over the world. The college has a lot of sports facilities which students can use in their spare time. There is also a wide range of recreational activities which students can participate in. The committee is concerned that many students are not taking advantage of all there is on offer.

You have been asked to write a leaflet which:
- informs the students about the facilities and activities that are available
- points out the benefits of taking up these opportunities
- encourages students to use the facilities and join in the activities.

Write the **text for the leaflet**.

5   An international group of business people is coming to your company for a one-day visit, in order to observe working practices. Your manager has asked you to write a letter to the leader of the group, including:
- a brief introduction to your company
- the programme for the day's visit
- your views on what the group will learn about good working practices from their visit.

Write your **letter**.

PAPER 3   ENGLISH IN USE (1 hour 30 minutes)

Part 1

For questions **1–15**, read the text below and then decide which answer on page **49** best fits each space. Indicate your answer **on the separate answer sheet**. The exercise begins with an example **(0)**.

Example:

0	A	B	C	D
	▬	▭	▭	▭

Driving from Beijing to Paris

'Every **(0)** ..... begins with a single step.' We might **(1)** ..... this proverb for the 16,000 km Beijing to Paris car rally, and say that every rally begins with a **(2)** ..... of the wheel. From China, several hundred courageous men and women will **(3)** ..... out for Paris in pursuit of what, for many, is likely to prove an impossible **(4)** .... Everybody is prepared for the worst and expects a high drop-out **(5)** ..... , especially on the rally's difficult first **(6)** ..... across central China and over the high mountain **(7)** ..... of the Himalayas. 'If twenty-five cars **(8)** ..... it to Paris, we'll be doing well,' says Philip Young, the rally organiser.

Now planned as an annual event, the first Beijing-Paris car rally took place in 1907. It was won by Prince Borghese, an Italian adventurer, who crossed the **(9)** ..... line just a few metres **(10)** ..... of the only other car to complete the race. Nowadays, not many people know about Prince Borghese, but at the time his achievement was **(11)** ..... as comparable to that of Marco Polo, who travelled from Venice to China in the thirteenth century.

According to the **(12)** ....., all the cars in the rally must be more than thirty years old, which means that the **(13)** ..... roads and high altitude are a **(14)** ..... test of both the cars and the drivers. A sense of adventure is essential. One driver said, 'Our **(15)** ..... is to have a good time, enjoy the experience and the magnificent scenery – and the adventure of a lifetime.'

---

0 **(A)** journey   **B** travel   **C** route   **D** way

1 **A** adapt   **B** moderate   **C** improve   **D** form

2 **A** revolution   **B** circle   **C** rotation   **D** turn

3 **A** head   **B** move   **C** set   **D** try

4 **A** vision   **B** fantasy   **C** hope   **D** dream

5 **A** rate   **B** number   **C** speed   **D** frequency

6 **A** period   **B** stage   **C** time   **D** round

7 **A** crossings   **B** passes   **C** directions   **D** passages

8 **A** get   **B** take   **C** have   **D** make

9 **A** closing   **B** final   **C** ending   **D** finishing

10 **A** forward   **B** ahead   **C** front   **D** advance

11 **A** thought   **B** referred   **C** regarded   **D** noted

12 **A** orders   **B** rules   **C** laws   **D** customs

13 **A** crude   **B** undeveloped   **C** broken   **D** rough

14 **A** firm   **B** strict   **C** severe   **D** grave

15 **A** aim   **B** target   **C** proposal   **D** intent

Part 2

For questions **16–30**, complete the following article by writing each missing word in the correct box on your answer sheet. **Use only one word for each space**. The exercise begins with an example **(0)**.

Example: | **0** | *been* | **0** |

Blue whales

Blue whales, the world's largest animals, have **(0)** ..... sighted again in British waters for the first time in **(16)** ..... least twenty years. Indications that a population of blue whales was inhabiting the waters west **(17)** ..... Scotland came for the first time from the United States Navy, **(18)** ..... surveillance system picked up the songs of a lot of different whales. American zoologists subsequently identified the blue whale song among **(19)** ..... .

Now marine biologist, Carol Booker, **(20)** ..... actually seen a blue whale there herself. She has no doubt about what she saw, because they have distinctive fins which are very small for **(21)** ..... size. She says, 'Worldwide they were almost extinct and **(22)** ..... seemed they had completely vanished from the North Atlantic, so you can imagine how I felt actually seeing **(23)** ..... ! However, it is certainly **(24)** ..... soon to say if it is an indication of a population recovery.' She goes **(25)** ..... to say, 'What it does show **(26)** ..... the importance of this area of the ocean for whales, and **(27)** ..... essential it is to control pollution of the seas.'

Bigger than **(28)** ..... dinosaur known to man, blue whales are the largest animals ever to **(29)** ..... lived on earth. A blue whale is more than six metres long at birth and, **(30)** ..... fully grown, its heart is the same height as a tall man and weighs as much as a horse.

Part 3

In **most** lines of the following text, there is **either** a spelling **or** a punctuation error. For each numbered line **31–46**, write the correctly spelt word or show the correct punctuation in the box on your answer sheet. **Some lines are correct.** Indicate these lines with a tick (✓) in the box. The exercise begins with three examples (**0**), (**00**) and (**000**).

Examples:	0	✓	0
	00	point where	00
	000	dominate	000

The guitar in Rock and Roll

0	In just over forty years, the guitar has risen from practical obscurity
00	to a point, where life would seem very strange without it. The first
000	instruments to domminate rock and roll were the piano and the tenor
31	saxophone, but it wasn't too long before the guitar caught-up.
32	Fashions in musical instruments may come and go, but the guitar
33	is here to stay. It is the perfect acompaniment to the human voice.
34	It is more portable than the piano, relativly inexpensive and readily
35	adaptible to almost any musical style. The learner guitarist of today
36	has one distinct advantage over his predecessor forty years, or so ago,
37	which is that the guitar he or she buys brand new will be perfectly
38	playable. Musicians are indebted to todays guitar makers for this.
39	Things were far thougher four decades ago. Many guitar stars started
40	out as mere mortals strugling to either buy or build their first guitar.
41	Much experimentation was involved, a lot of it crazy and futile. The
42	appeal of rock and roll led to desparate measures on the part of Britain's
43	youth, as they attemted to own the types of guitar they saw their new
44	heroes' playing on television. Good guitars were expensive, but people
45	with construction skills and helpful parents were able to make almost
46	the real thing, although many efforts to build guitars had disastrious results.

Part 4

For questions **47–61**, read the texts on pages **52** and **53**. Use the words in the boxes to the right of the texts to form **one** word that fits in the same numbered space in the texts. Write the new word in the correct box on your answer sheet. The exercise begins with an example (**0**).

Example:

0	*obsession*	0

EXTRACT FROM AN ARTICLE

Our passion for chocolate

Some experts believe that the reason for our **(0)** ..... with chocolate lies in its chemical content, but most tend to put its attraction down to psychology. It has not been **(47)** ..... proven that the chemical substances contained in chocolate lead to our need for it. The **(48)** ..... , the flavour, texture and calories make it **(49)** ..... . Some people are born with a **(50)** ..... for sweet things and chocolate readily meets this need because of its **(51)** ..... in every corner of the world. We grow to associate it with rewards, gifts and love. We also use it for emotional comfort. Most bars contain only a small percentage of cocoa solids. Those who are fans of 'real chocolate', which can contain up to 70%, claim it is a much **(52)** ..... option, and less **(53)** ..... .

(0)	**OBSESS**
(47)	SCIENCE
(48)	SWEET
(49)	DESIRE
(50)	PREFER
(51)	AVAILABLE
(52)	HEALTH
(53)	ADDICT

LEAFLET

The Cheltenham Park Hotel

If you are looking for a hotel designed for **(54)** ..... , which is also **(55)** ..... priced, your search may be over. Situated in a quiet, leafy square, we are five minutes' walk from the town centre and ten minutes from the park and sports centre. All sixty-five of our **(56)** ..... bedrooms, many of them enjoying views of the surrounding countryside, have been **(57)** ..... designed and furnished. Each room has satellite colour TV and telephone. Our restaurant, with its **(58)** ..... selection of award-winning international cuisine and carefully **(59)** ..... menus, ensures that each meal is an absolutely **(60)** ..... experience. Whether you are here for business or pleasure, your visit will be **(61)** ..... .

(54) RELAX
(55) REASON
(56) SPACE
(57) TASTE
(58) IMAGINE
(59) CHOOSE
(60) FORGET
(61) MEMORY

Part 5

For questions **62–74**, read the following memo from an airline executive to his secretary regarding a passenger who has lost his luggage. Use the information in it to complete the numbered gaps in the formal letter written to the passenger. Write the new words in the correct boxes **on your answer sheet**. The words you need **do not occur** in the memo. **Use no more than two words for each gap.** The exercise begins with an example (**0**).

Example:

0	communication	0

MEMO

TO: Sally Roget

FROM: Dave Collins

I've just had a message on my answer phone from Mr Crystal about his missing bags. Could you write to him to confirm the situation as it now stands. Tell him that we know that he checked them in at the airport and that he has a baggage ticket showing this. I was pleased to hear him say that the people in the lost luggage office were very helpful when his bags failed to turn up.

I told him in a previous letter that his luggage was still missing. Unfortunately, nothing has changed. Please tell him that I'm very sorry, but even though we've made a thorough search, we still can't find it. Please tell him we're incredibly sorry about all this. We will, of course, be making it up to him financially. However, we do need to know what was in the suitcases and roughly how much it's worth. If he has any questions, he should give me a call as soon as possible.

FORMAL LETTER

Thank you for your recent **(0)** ..... in which you refer to the unfortunate problem with your luggage. I would like to update you on the situation at **(62)** ..... . We **(63)** ..... that your bags were checked in at the airport and that you have the **(64)** ..... support this. We are also pleased that you mention the fact that our Lost Luggage **(65)** ..... were extremely helpful when your luggage did **(66)** ..... on the carousel at the airport. I **(67)** ..... you in previous correspondence that your luggage had not been found. Unfortunately, the situation remains **(68)** ..... . I regret, therefore, that despite having **(69)** ..... this matter extensively, we have been unable to **(70)** ..... either of your two pieces of luggage. We would like to offer our apologies for this most unfortunate incident. In order to **(71)** ..... you we require precise information about the **(72)** ..... of your suitcases, with their **(73)** ..... values. Should you have any further queries, please do not hesitate to **(74)** ..... me.

Part 6

For questions **75–80**, read the following text and then choose from the list **A–I** given below the best phrase to fill each of the spaces. Indicate your answers on the separate answer sheet. Each correct phrase may only be used once. **Some of the suggested answers do not fit at all.**

Climbing Big Ben

It has long been possible to climb Big Ben, the famous clock that stands outside Parliament, but few visitors to London know this. Brian Davis, claims it is the most accurate clock in the world and he should know, **(75)** ..... .

He greets his tour group at the foot of the clock tower, where 334 steps separate them from the top or 'belfry'. It is 11.30 a.m. and he aims to be there when Big Ben strikes noon. Some people have brought ear plugs but are quickly reassured that they won't be needed. The bell is loud **(76)** ..... .

We drag ourselves up the first 114 steps and into a little museum. This is the clock tower prison room. It looks very inhospitable **(77)** ..... . We continue to tackle the steps in stages and reach the belfry five minutes before midday. Here Brian points out that, strictly speaking, Big Ben is the name of the bell **(78)** ..... .

When Big Ben booms, I don't put my fingers in my ears because I want to experience the full might of the noise. Imagine a clap of thunder breaking directly over your head **(79)** ..... . I could feel it in my teeth. Above the clock face is a mechanism, controlled, Brian explains, not by technology but by a pile of old coins. And with that he leads us down again, a man who clearly enjoys **(80)** ..... .

A and so we move on and up quickly
B having taken such a long time to build
C and then repeated several more times
D having spent so much time talking about it
E having a job in such an important place
F but it is not really that uncomfortable
G and is not like any of the other clocks
H having a sound that is difficult to hear
I and not the clock as people often believe

PAPER 4   LISTENING (approximately 45 minutes)

Part 1

You will hear part of a radio programme in which an expert on theatre history is talking about the life of a famous actress called Helen Perry. For questions **1–8**, complete the sentences.

You will hear the recording twice.

The common view that acting was an unsuitable career for a woman was shared by **[1]**

Helen admitted that her greatest problems in acting involved **[2]**

In her fifties, Helen had to have a dangerous **[3]** which saved her career.

Helen's broad popularity reflects her skill as both a **[4]** and a classical actress.

Helen was so popular that a brand of **[5]** was named after her.

Evidence of Helen's skill as a writer can be found in some of the **[6]** that she wrote.

We can get an idea of the quality of her later performances from **[7]** of the time.

What pleased Helen most was the attention she received from **[8]**

Part 2

You will hear a talk given by Norma Tainton, a journalist who writes reviews of restaurants. For questions **9–16**, complete the sentences.

Listen very carefully as you will hear the recording ONCE only.

FOOD WRITER

Norma's reviews appear in newspapers and ⬚ **9**

The type of food which Norma especially likes eating is ⬚ **10**

Norma says she aims to try dishes which are

⬚ **11** in some way.

Generally, Norma depends on her guests for information about the

⬚ **12**

Norma says she sometimes needs to make a note of

⬚ **13** during a meal.

When considering prices, she is keen that her readers get

⬚ **14** in restaurants.

Norma prefers to avoid making ⬚ **15** about restaurants.

Norma denies that she gets

⬚ **16** when she goes to a restaurant.

Part 3

You will hear a radio interview with the writer, Tom Davies. For questions **17–22**, choose the correct answer **A**, **B**, **C** or **D**.

You will hear the recording twice.

17 How does Tom feel now about being a writer?

    A   It is no longer as exciting as it was.
    B   He used to get more pleasure from it.
    C   He is still surprised when it goes well.
    D   It is less difficult to do these days.

18 How does Tom feel about the idea for a novel before he begins writing it?

    A   He lacks confidence in himself.
    B   He is very secretive about it.
    C   He likes to get reactions to it.
    D   He is uncertain how it will develop.

19 Tom's behaviour when beginning a new novel can best be described as

    A   determined.
    B   enthusiastic.
    C   impulsive.
    D   unpredictable.

20 What does Tom say happens to writers as they get older and better known?

    A   Their friends are more honest with them.
    B   Publishers are less likely to criticise them.
    C   They get less objective about their own work.
    D   They find it harder to accept criticism.

21 What does Tom admit about his novels?

    A They are not completely imaginary.
    B They are open to various interpretations.
    C They do not reflect his personal views.
    D They do not make very good films.

22 What did Tom feel about the first film he was involved in making?

    A He enjoyed being part of a team.
    B He found it much too stressful.
    C He earned too little money from it.
    D He was reassured by how easy it was.

Part 4

You will hear five short extracts in which different people are reading from their autobiographies.

You will hear the recording twice. While you listen you must complete both tasks.

TASK ONE

For questions **23–27**, match the extracts as you hear them with what each speaker is saying, listed **A–H**.

A   I made up my mind about something.

B   I had a piece of luck.

C   My popularity started to decline.

D   I received some bad publicity.

E   I achieved an ambition.

F   My attitude to fame changed.

G   I made a mistake.

H   I turned down an opportunity.

Speaker 1 | 23 |

Speaker 2 | 24 |

Speaker 3 | 25 |

Speaker 4 | 26 |

Speaker 5 | 27 |

TASK TWO

For questions **28–32**, match the extracts with the feeling each speaker expresses, listed **A–H**.

A   regret

B   relief

C   annoyance

D   optimism

E   anxiety

F   embarrassment

G   indifference

H   disappointment

Speaker 1 | 28 |

Speaker 2 | 29 |

Speaker 3 | 30 |

Speaker 4 | 31 |

Speaker 5 | 32 |

PAPER 5   SPEAKING (15 minutes for pairs of candidates, 23 minutes for groups of three)

(This test is also suitable for groups of three candidates; this only occurs as the last test of a session where a centre has an uneven number of candidates.)

There are two examiners. One (the interlocutor) conducts the test, providing you with the necessary materials and explaining what you have to do. The other examiner (the assessor) is introduced to you, but then takes no further part in the interaction.

Part 1 (3 minutes for pairs of candidates, 5 minutes for groups of three)

The interlocutor first asks you and your partner(s) a few questions. You are then asked to find out some information about each other, on topics such as hobbies, interests, future plans, etc. You are then asked further questions by the interlocutor.

Part 2 (4 minutes for pairs of candidates, 6 minutes for groups of three)

You are each given the opportunity to talk for about a minute, and to comment briefly after your partner has spoken.

The interlocutor gives you a set of pictures and asks you to talk about them for about one minute. The interlocutor also asks you to let your partner(s) see your pictures.

Your partner / one of your partners is then given another set of pictures to look at and this candidate talks about these pictures for about one minute. The interlocutor also asks this candidate to let their partner(s) see their pictures.

If a group of three candidates is being examined, the interlocutor gives another set of pictures to the third candidate to look at. This candidate talks about these pictures for about a minute. The interlocutor also asks this candidate to let their partners see their pictures.

When you have all had your turn, the interlocutor asks you to look at each other's pictures again and answer together another question, which relates to all the pictures.

Part 3 (approximately 4 minutes for pairs of candidates, 6 minutes for groups of three)

In this part of the test you and your partner(s) are asked to talk together. The interlocutor places a new set of pictures on the table in front of you. This stimulus provides the basis for a discussion. The interlocutor then explains what you have to do.

Part 4 (approximately 4 minutes for pairs of candidates, 6 minutes for groups of three)

The interlocutor asks some further questions, which leads to a more general discussion of what you have talked about in Part 3. You may comment on the answers of your partner(s) if you wish.

Test 3

PAPER 1 READING (1 hour 15 minutes)

✗ **Part 1**

Answer questions **1–12** by referring to the newspaper article about emotional intelligence on page
65. Indicate your answers **on the separate answer sheet**.

For questions **1–12**, answer by choosing from the sections of the article (**A–D**) on page 65.
Some of the choices may be required more than once.

In which section are the following mentioned?

the significance of emotional intelligence in work that is challenging	**1**..........
increased accuracy in the way emotional intelligence is described	**2**..........
the means by which we are assessed at work having become more comprehensive	**3**..........
the fact that emotional intelligence can be combined with other skills to improve people's ability to cope at work	**4**..........
areas in which emotional intelligence cannot be expected to offer solutions	**5**..........
people having succeeded despite inadequacies in emotional intelligence	**6**..........
the assumption that people have the academic skills to perform their jobs well	**7**..........
the negative effect that a lack of emotional intelligence can have on a person's other skills	**8**..........
the means of predicting who will excel in the workplace	**9**.........
the reason why organisations promote emotional intelligence in the workplace	**10**..........
misconceptions about what emotional intelligence involves	**11**..........
the kind of staff relations that ensure an organisation has an advantage over its rivals	**12**..........

Emotional Intelligence – The Key to Success

Daniel Goleman examines the 'people skills' that are essential for a place at the top of your profession

A

The rules for work are changing. We are being judged by a new yardstick – not just by how clever we are, or by our training and expertise, but also by how well we handle ourselves and each other. This yardstick is increasingly used in choosing who will be hired and who will not, who will be passed over and who will not. The new rules can be used to indicate who is likely to become a star performer and who is most prone to mediocrity. And, no matter what field we work in currently, they measure the traits that are crucial to our marketability for future jobs. These rules have little to do with what we were told at school was important. The ability to do well in examinations is largely irrelevant to this standard. The new measure takes it for granted that we all have enough intellectual ability and technical know-how to do our jobs. It focuses instead on social skills and personal qualities, such as initiative and empathy, adaptability and persuasiveness – the 'people skills' that make up what is now commonly referred to as emotional intelligence.

B

In a time when few guarantees of job security have led to the very concept of a 'job' being rapidly replaced by 'portable skills', personal qualities begin to play an important role in the workplace. Talked about loosely for decades under a variety of names, from 'character' and 'personality' to 'soft skills', there is, at last, a more precise understanding of these human talents as well as a new name for them. 'Emotional intelligence' is generally defined as the ability to monitor and regulate one's own and others' feelings, and to use feelings to guide thought and action. In our work-life it comprises five basic elements: self-awareness, self-regulation, motivation, empathy and adeptness in social relationships. There is a common assumption that it simply means 'being nice'. However, at strategic moments it may demand not 'being nice', but rather, for example, bluntly confronting someone with the uncomfortable truth. Nor does emotional intelligence mean giving free rein to feelings – 'letting it all hang out'. Rather, it means managing feelings so that they are expressed appropriately and effectively, enabling people to work together smoothly towards their common goal.

C

More and more businesses are seeing that encouraging emotional intelligence skills is a vital component of management philosophy. And the less straightforward the job, the more emotional intelligence matters – if only because a deficiency in these abilities can hinder the use of whatever technical expertise or intellect a person may have. There are many examples of people who have risen to the top notwithstanding flaws in emotional intelligence, but as work becomes more complex and collaborative, companies where people work together best have a competitive edge. In the new workplace, with its emphasis on teamwork and a strong customer orientation, this crucial set of emotional competencies is becoming increasingly essential for excellence in every job and in every part of the world.

D

Whereas one's IQ undergoes few changes, emotional intelligence continues to develop as we go through life and learn from our experiences; our competence in it can keep growing. In fact, studies that have measured people's emotional intelligence through the years show that most people grow more adept at handling their own emotions and impulses, at motivating themselves and at honing their empathy and social adroitness. There is an old-fashioned word for this growth in emotional intelligence: maturity. Not only can emotional intelligence be learnt, but individually we can add these skills to our tool kit for survival. This is especially relevant at a time when it seems a contradiction to put the words 'job' and 'stability' together. Emotional intelligence is no magic formula for uncompetitive organisations, no guarantee of more market share or a healthier bottom line. But if the human ingredient is ignored, then nothing else works as well as it might.

Part 2

For questions **13–18**, you must choose which of the extracts **A–G** on page **67** fit into the numbered gaps in the following magazine article. There is one extra paragraph which does not fit in any of the gaps. Indicate your answers **on the separate answer sheet**.

✕ Beginner Takes All

Even before it was published, *The Horse Whisperer* was the hottest book of the year. A first novel by British screenwriter Nicholas Evans, it has earned its author record-breaking sums. He talks here about his inspiration and his triumph

The first months of the year were not kind to Nicholas Evans, screenwriter, producer and aspiring director. The year began badly when *Life and Limb*, a film project he had been working on for months, fell through 'almost overnight'. His disappointment mingled with stomach-churning worry: it had been two years since he had earned any money and the promise of that film had been the only buffer between him and an increasingly irate bank manager.

13

Although he was acting very much on impulse, the seeds for the story had been with him for some time, <u>sown</u> by a farrier he met on Dartmoor while staying with a friend. The farrier had told him the story of a docile horse that had turned, no one knew why, into a fiend. Its owners were desperate until they heard of a gypsy who, simply by talking to the animal, transformed its temperament in a matter of hours. Such men, the farrier said, were known as 'horse whisperers'.

14

'It was a funny time,' he says now. 'I was observing people, but essentially I was alone and I really felt as though my life was falling apart. I'd tried for ten years to make a go of it as a film-maker, and here I was, hugely in debt and wondering how I was going to feed the children, and thinking maybe it was all just folly.'

15

When pushed, he ventured that Evans might get $30,000 as an advance on the book. 'I had in mind how much I needed to pay off a bit of the overdraft and keep us going, and it was more than that. I'd spent seven months on *The Horse Whisperer,* and there were at least another two to go. $30,000 was a really difficult figure. I was also advised to write a 12-page synopsis of the remainder of the book.'

16

The events that followed have become publishing history. Within a week – a week of hotly contested auctions – the novel had been sold to Transworld Publications in the UK for $550,000 and to Delacorte in the US for $3.15 million, both record-breaking advances for a first novel.

17

As they all agreed to this sum, it was decided that they should each 'pitch' to Evans. And so, one night in October, he sat in his study while four great film-makers rang, one after the other, to beg for the privilege of paying $3 million for an unfinished novel. Evans told me all this as we sat drinking coffee on a wooden verandah perched above the leafy garden of his home. He said that he had since turned down an offer to write the screenplay of *The Horse Whisperer.*

18

He would be involved, he said, but at arm's length. The success of his novel had inevitably brought forth the offer of new backing for *Life and Limb,* but he was no longer sure that he wanted to make it. 'I think that I would be foolish not to write another novel,' he said.

A Evans' imagination was captured. He began researching the subject with a view to writing a screenplay – he was, after all, a film-maker. But disillusionment with the film world following the demise of *Life and Limb* prompted him to write the story as a book. And so throughout the spring he drove across the US, stopping at ranches and learning about horses and the men who work with them.

B 'It's all been such a fairy tale so far, I don't want to spoil it. Writing at that level is a very tough business, and I don't want to become an employee of these people who I like and who have paid me so much money. I'd hate to find myself writing a draft or two and then have them say, "Thanks Nick, but now we'll bring in so-and-so".'

C 'We couldn't believe it; we sat there with our jaws gaping. We'd never sent the manuscript to New York, we still don't know how it got there,' Evans says. Nor did they send it to Hollywood, but within that same week the major studios were fighting over it. 'My agent in the UK wisely involved an agent over there and when he phoned us to say, "I think we can get $3 million outright," we laughed in disbelief.'

D As a screenwriter, he had yearned for the freedom of novelists and, when he had it, found himself 'in the middle of this immense and terrifying plain without the support of screenplay rules to guide me.' But he carries us smoothly through. Even so, he remains baffled as to why the story has captured imaginations in the mind-blowing way that it has.

E He thought that again towards the end of August, by which time he had returned home and written the first half of the book. 'At that point the bank manager was getting really very heavy with us, and I needed to know whether it was worth going on. I plucked up the courage to show it to a friend who was a literary agent; he read it and said it was "fine".'

F A wise man, finding himself in Evans' position, would have got a job. He could have gone back to being a television executive, or begun a television project that had been on hold. Instead, he made a decision that most people, Evans included, would consider insane. He bought a ticket to America and set off for three months to research his first novel.

G In October, together with the first two hundred pages of the novel, this was sent to seven UK publishers on the eve of their departure for the annual spending spree at the internationally renowned Frankfurt Book Fair. Within days his agent was on the telephone to report that he had just turned down the first offer of $75,000. 'I said, "You what?" And he said, "It's OK, I just sense something is happening".'

Part 3

Read the following magazine article and answer questions **19–24** on page **69**. **On your answer sheet**, indicate the letter **A**, **B**, **C** or **D** against the number of each question, **19–24**. Give only one answer to each question.

✕ The Cabinet-Maker

Charles Hurst makes a living from perfectly crafted furniture.
Joanna Watt *meets him*

Charles Hurst gives the impression of being a man in a hurry. I arrive at his workshop, tucked under a railway arch in East London, and am greeted with a quick handshake and the words: 'Well, fire away then!' Whether this brusqueness is real or a front hiding a shy streak is not immediately apparent. But a glance around the workshop reveals that Hurst is obviously busy, with good reason not to waste a minute of his time.

The arched space is full of half-made pieces of furniture and planks of wood in an amazing array of natural colours. Hurst has been a cabinet-maker for ten years and has built up a very nice reputation for himself. His order book is always full for several months in advance, despite the fact that he does not really promote himself. Word has spread that if you want a decent cupboard or table, bookcase or kitchen units, Hurst is your man.

Of course, finding a furniture-maker is not that taxing a task. Wherever you live in the countryside, the craft is alive and well. But finding a cabinet-maker who prides himself on making beautifully crafted furniture with clean, simple lines is less easy. 'There are few real cabinet-makers now. People call themselves furniture-makers,' Hurst says wearily. As a craftsman who sets himself exacting standards, he is continually disappointed by some contemporary furniture. 'I am amazed by what some furniture-makers get away with, and saddened by what people will put up with.' He rails against shoddy, mass-produced furniture, and craftsmen who churn out second-rate pieces.

Such a quest for perfection is obviously a key to Hurst's success. That and his talent. This man is not coy about his ability. Indeed, his blatant self-confidence is as surprising as his initial brusque manner. 'I have a huge natural ability,' he says, with a deadpan expression. 'I have always been good at making things.' If it were not for the self-deprecating mood into which he slipped towards the end of our interview, I would have believed his conceit to be wholly genuine.

Hurst is self-taught. So how did he learn his craft? 'I asked the right questions and picked it all up,' he says nonchalantly. Almost all of his commissions come from private individuals ('I used to do some commercial work for companies but it was soul-destroying'). Some clients have returned time and again. 'You end up doing the whole of their house. That is very satisfying.' But he is honest enough to admit that relationships with clients do not always run smoothly. 'The most infuriating clients are those who don't know what they want, and then decide they do when it's too late … my favourite clients are the exacting ones.'

If Hurst has every reason to be pleased with himself, he is also gracious in his praise for others – where it is due. With a sudden shot of modesty, he says: 'There are people far better than me. I can admire other people. After all, I wasn't trained at Parnham' (the leading college of furniture design). However, he is also unremittingly critical of those craftsmen who 'are trying to be artists and take a year to make one piece.' He also has little time for degree shows, in which students exhibit their work but at the same time are 'trying to make fashion statements. That can be pretentious. A piece of furniture is not about making a statement. It has to be something that people really can use.'

Confident Hurst may be, even brusque, but you could never call him or his work pretentious. Indeed, his parting shot displays a welcome down-to-earth approach to his craft and a streak of humility strangely at odds with his earlier self-confidence. 'After all, I am only making furniture,' he says as I make my exit.

19 When she arrived at the workshop, the writer

    A was not sure if her first impression of Hurst was accurate.
    B was offended by the way Hurst introduced himself.
    C thought that Hurst was pretending to have a lot to do.
    D thought it was obvious that Hurst did not want to speak to her.

20 Hurst has few problems selling his furniture because he

    A advertises locally.
    B is known to be a skilled craftsman.
    C uses only natural materials.
    D has a reputation for being fair.

21 What does Hurst think has led to the decline in the craft of cabinet-making?

    A It is a difficult skill to learn.
    B It is only popular in rural areas.
    C Consumers will accept poor quality furniture.
    D Simple designs do not appeal to modern tastes.

22 The writer says that when Hurst describes his 'talent', he

    A has a tendency to exaggerate.
    B reveals a natural sense of humour.
    C becomes more animated than he usually is.
    D appears more arrogant than he really is.

23 Hurst believes that it is essential for craftsmen to

    A create original furniture.
    B exhibit to a wide audience.
    C produce functional designs.
    D invest extra time in perfecting their work.

24 The writer's final impression of Hurst is that he

    A has an unusual attitude to his work.
    B believes in the special nature of his work.
    C enjoys being interviewed about his work.
    D has the ability to put his work into perspective.

Part 4

Answer questions **25–45** by referring to the newspaper article on pages **71–72** about scientific biographies. Indicate your answers **on the separate answer sheet**.

For questions **25–45**, answer by choosing from the sections of the article **(A–D)**. Some of the choices may be required more than once.

Which section mentions the following?

the continuing general scarcity of biographies of scientists	**25**..........
an increase in the number of ways scientists are featured in the media	**26**..........
certain parallels between the lives of two people	**27**..........
the fact that science can become accessible to the non-scientist	**28**..........
the changing nature of books about scientists	**29**..........
an attitude which is common to scientists and people working in the book trade	**30**..........
the lack of trust people sometimes have in scientists	**31**..........
someone whose scientific research went much further than others had believed possible	**32**..........
someone whose life mirrors historical developments	**33**..........
biographies which include the less positive aspects of a scientist's life	**34**..........
the lessons to be taken from someone else's life	**35**..........
growing public interest in the everyday lives of brilliant people	**36**..........
the greatest difficulty in writing the biography of a scientist	**37**..........
someone who was modest about the interest of their own life to others	**38**..........
an achievement that would gain more general recognition if it were in another field	**39**..........
the fact that most people's comprehension of science does not go beyond the basics	**40**..........
the idea that people who study in different disciplines cannot be of interest to one another	**41**..........
the fact that people are not ashamed if they are unaware of the names of great scientists	**42**..........
an attitude which dissuades people from following a scientific career	**43**..........
an expectation that was too optimistic	**44**..........
the absence of personal information in most scientific biographies	**45**..........

Dorothy *who?*

The only British woman scientist to win the Nobel prize should be a household name in her own country, says Georgina Ferry, but she is little known

A

For the past four years, I have been subjecting friends and acquaintances to the Dorothy Hodgkin test. It's very simple: when asked what I am working on, I tell them I am writing the first biography of Dorothy Hodgkin. If their eyes light up, and they say things like 'Surely there's one already?' they have passed.

Why should people in Britain know about Dorothy Hodgkin? The fact that she is the only British woman scientist to have won a Nobel prize ought to be enough. Anyone who held the same distinction in literature would be a household name. But Hodgkin, who died in 1994, was a remarkable individual by any standards, as many-faceted as the crystals she studied. Her life reflects some of the greatest upheavals of the 20th century: among them, the advancement of women's education and the globalisation of science.

When I began my research, I set out to read some scientific biographies. One of Hodgkin's friends recommended a new biography of Linus Pauling. Pauling was a close friend and contemporary of Hodgkin, worked in the same branch of science and shared a commitment to campaigning against nuclear weapons. I hurried to the main bookshop in the university town where I live, only to discover that not a single biography of Pauling was on the shelves. I now realise I was naive to be surprised that Pauling was not deemed sufficiently interesting to British readers, even though he was the most influential chemist of the 20th century and a winner of Nobel prizes for both chemistry and peace.

B

Even scientists themselves have doubted the value of the scientific biography. 'The lives of scientists, considered as Lives, almost always make dull reading', wrote the late Peter Medawar, another Nobel laureate, who laid most of the scientific groundwork that now makes organ transplants possible.

If scientists propagate this negative view, it is hardly surprising if publishers and booksellers share it. Treating scientists differently from everybody else as biographical subjects is one of the outstanding symptoms of the 'two cultures' mentality, the belief that there is an unbridgeable divide of understanding between the arts and sciences, still prevalent in the literary world. Few but the towering giants of science make it into the biography sections of bookshops.

Of course it is nonsense to say scientists, as a group, lead less interesting lives than artists and writers, or actors, or politicians. For some, the fastidiousness involved in maintaining scientific credibility extends to any kind of media appearance. A leading geneticist once told me he was happy to be interviewed about his work, but did not want to be quoted directly or photographed, because he did not want to be perceived as 'self-promoting'.

C

The avoidance of the personal conveys a false impression of the enterprise of science that discourages young people from joining in, and fosters more public suspicion than it dispels.

Fortunately, gaps are appearing in the smokescreen. Contemporary scientists now regularly appear in the public eye in contexts other than the straightforward scientific interview. For instance, Professor Richard Dawkins presents prizes to winners of a TV quiz, and geneticist Steve Jones advertises cars on television. No doubt these activities have raised eyebrows in laboratories but they have done more to make scientists recognisable as people than any number of academic papers.

The publishing world is also undergoing a transformation. Scientific biographies and autobiographies, if they appeared at all, used to be rather scholarly but dull and over-reverent. The life which the scientist in question led outside work – marriage, children, things most people regard as fairly central to their existence – was often dismissed in a couple of paragraphs. That changed with Richard Feynman's *Surely You're Joking, Mr Feynman?*, the hilarious and affecting memoir of a man who also happened to be one of the century's greatest theoretical physicists.

More recently, even the greatest names in science, such as Isaac Newton, Charles Darwin, Albert Einstein and Marie Curie have been allowed to appear with all their flaws clearly visible. To the reader, it does not matter that Einstein's relationship with his family is 'irrelevant' to his General Theory of Relativity. The question of how creative genius copes with emotional ups and downs, trivial practicalities, the social demands of ordinary life, is absorbing in its own right.

D

Dorothy Hodgkin was devoted to her scientific work. Her most important successes were solving the structure of penicillin and vitamin B12, which won her the Nobel prize for chemistry in 1964, and of insulin, which her group solved in 1969. In each case she pushed the technique into realms of complexity others deemed unreachable at the time.

But she also had three children to whom she was devoted and was married to a frequently absent husband with a career as a historian. Her personal life is not strictly relevant to her work as a scientist, but surely we can all learn from her capacity to unite the disparate threads of her life into a coherent whole. There is much in her life of universal interest, but it would be disloyal of me to imply that this does not include the science itself. Scientific inquiry was the passion of Hodgkin's life, as it has to be for any successful scientist.

How to communicate the nature of this passion is the hardest task for the scientific biographer. Most readers are not equipped with enough fundamental scientific concepts to grasp more complex ideas without a lot of explanation. Understanding scientific ideas is not really any more difficult than reading Shakespeare or learning a foreign language – it just takes application. It is sad to think that educated people, who would be embarrassed if they failed to recognise the name of some distinguished literary or artistic figure, continue to live in happy ignorance of the rich heritage represented by scientists such as Dorothy Hodgkin.

PAPER 2 WRITING (2 hours)

Part 1

1   You are studying at a college in Britain. A television company wishes to feature this college in a programme it is making about language learning institutions. The college principal has given you the TV company's letter and has asked you to write them a proposal, suggesting what the film should include.

Read the extract from the TV company's letter below, with your comments, and on page **74**, the memo from the principal, together with the notes you have made about the possible people to interview. Then, **using the information appropriately**, write a proposal for the TV company, explaining which aspects of the college should be filmed, who should be interviewed and why.

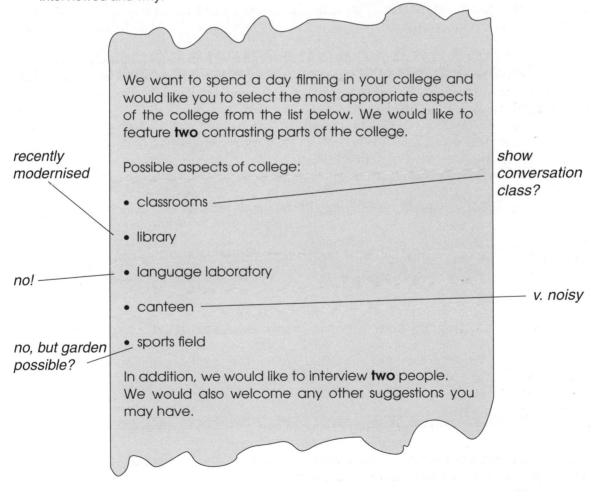

We want to spend a day filming in your college and would like you to select the most appropriate aspects of the college from the list below. We would like to feature **two** contrasting parts of the college.

recently modernised

Possible aspects of college:

show conversation class?

- classrooms

- library

- language laboratory

no!

- canteen

v. noisy

no, but garden possible?

- sports field

In addition, we would like to interview **two** people. We would also welcome any other suggestions you may have.

MEMO

From: The principal

Re: Request from TV company

Can you prepare a proposal regarding the TV company's request? Select what you think should be filmed and explain why. As for the two interviews, three students, Kim, Peter and Maria, have said they would be interested. It might be a good idea to invite a teacher. What do you think? Could you make a choice and explain why it would be good to film the two people you select? We must make sure the programme gives a positive impression of the college.

Thanks

M Smith

Possible interviews?

Kim — shy, but English good

Peter — been here <u>ages</u>, knows everything!

Maria — chatty and confident, been on lots of college trips

How about a teacher? Mr Brown would be good ...

Now write your **proposal** for the TV company as outlined on page **73** (approximately 250 words). You should use your own words as far as possible.

Part 2

Choose **one** of the following writing tasks. Your answer should follow exactly the instructions given. Write approximately 250 words.

2   You see this announcement in an international student magazine.

Youth Matters

We are preparing a special edition of our magazine dedicated to the problems that affect young people in different countries today – in particular, those relating to work, education or the environment. Write us an article about the most important aspects of **one** of these issues facing young people in **your** country today.

Write your **article**.

3   A friend of your family is applying for a job with a travel company as a tourist guide for English speaking tourists visiting your country. The company has asked you to provide a character reference for your friend.

The reference should indicate how long you have known the person. It must also include a detailed description of the person's character and the reasons why he or she would be suitable for the job.

Write the **reference**.

4   You see this announcement in an English language magazine.

COMPETITION

Think about the place where you live, work or study. Is there a leisure facility which you think it needs? An art gallery? A sports centre? A multi-screen cinema? Or something else?
Write to us and tell us about **one** new leisure facility you would like to see.

You should:
- say what leisure facility you would like and why you think it is needed
- describe in detail what you would like the leisure facility to provide
- explain which groups of people in your community would most benefit from this facility.

The best entry will win two theatre tickets.

Write your **competition entry**.

5   You have been asked by your manager to write a leaflet for new employees, covering aspects of health and safety in your company.

You should mention the following points:
- what types of equipment are used in your company
- how to use them safely
- where to go and what to do if there is an emergency.

Write the **text for the leaflet**.

PAPER 3   ENGLISH IN USE (1 hour 30 minutes)

Part 1

For questions **1–15**, read the text below and then decide which answer on page **77** best fits each space. Indicate your answer **on the separate answer sheet**. The exercise begins with an example **(0)**.

Example: | 0 | A ▬   B ▭   C ▭   D ▭ |

Smart shoes

Smart shoes that **(0)** ..... their size throughout the day could soon be available. A prototype of such a shoe has already been produced and a commercial **(1)** ..... may be in production within a few years. The shoe contains sensors that constantly **(2)** ..... the amount of **(3)** ..... left in it. If the foot has become too large, a tiny valve opens and the shoe **(4)** ..... slightly. The entire control system is about 5mm square and is **(5)** ..... inside the shoe. This radical shoe **(6)** ..... a need because the volume of the **(7)** ..... foot can change by as much as 8% during the course of the day. The system is able to learn about the wearer's feet and **(8)** ..... up a picture of the size of his or her feet throughout the day. It will allow the shoes to change in size by up to 8% so that they always fit **(9)** ..... . They are obviously more comfortable and less likely to **(10)** ..... blisters. From an athlete's point of view, they can help improve **(11)** ..... a little, and that is why the first **(12)** ..... for the system is likely to be in a sports shoe.

Eventually, this system will find a **(13)** ..... in other household items, from beds that automatically change to fit the person sleeping in them, to power tools that **(14)** ..... themselves to the user's hand for better grip. There is no reason why the system couldn't be adapted for use in hundreds of consumer **(15)** ..... .

---

0 (A) adjust   B fit   C reform   D move

1 A assortment   B version   C style   D variety

2 A prove   B confirm   C inspect   D check

3 A room   B gap   C area   D emptiness

4 A amplifies   B develops   C expands   D increases

5 A located   B sited   C established   D laid

6 A detects   B finds   C meets   D faces

7 A average   B general   C usual   D medium

8 A build   B pick   C grow   D set

9 A exactly   B absolutely   C completely   D totally

10 A provoke   B form   C initiate   D cause

11 A achievement   B performance C success   D winning

12 A purpose   B exercise   C use   D operation

13 A function   B part   C way   D place

14 A shape   B change   C respond   D convert

15 A commodities   B possessions C goods   D objects

Part 2

For questions **16–30**, complete the following article by writing each missing word in the correct box on your answer sheet. **Use only one word for each space**. The exercise begins with an example (**0**).

Example:

0	to	0

Central Park

If you have the chance **(0)** ..... take a walk through Central Park in New York, you will get a quick tour of the wide range of cultures and people who live in the city. **(16)** ..... man speeds along on a racing bike singing **(17)** ..... the top of his voice, **(18)** ..... dances to the beat of techno music coming from a tape recorder.

Central Park, the first public park built in America, allows for just about **(19)** ..... conceivable leisure activity in a rectangle of just over one and a half square kilometres. But it may **(20)** ..... that its best use is for the most entertaining sport in New York – people watching. Visitors can have **(21)** ..... better introduction to the diversity of New York than a stroll in this park.

Central Park did not always embrace **(22)** ..... a variety of human life. Having won a competition for the park's design in 1858, Frederick Law Olmsted and Calvert Vaux saw the place as an oasis of calm in a disorderly city. The idea **(23)** ..... to create a place where the upper-class citizens of the city could take gentle exercise **(24)** ..... being disturbed. However, the park authorities never managed to enforce **(25)** ..... regime of order. Olmsted **(26)** ..... been determined to create the illusion of the countryside in the heart of New York. The fact that skyscrapers are now visible **(27)** ..... the tops of the park's tallest trees **(28)** ...... certainly have horrified him. But this contrast between country and city landscape is **(29)** ..... gives the park **(30)** ..... very own special charm.

Part 3

In **most** lines of the following text, there is **either** a spelling **or** a punctuation error. For each numbered line **31–46**, write the correctly spelt word or show the correct punctuation in the box on your answer sheet. **Some lines are correct.** Indicate these lines with a tick (✓) in the box. The exercise begins with three examples (**0**), (**00**) and (**000**).

Examples:	0	connected	0
	00	✓	00
	000	Isles. Records	000

An old tradition

0	Ceremonies conected with natural springs of water or wells are very
00	old European customs, which now only survive in a few places in the
000	British Isles Records indicate that decorating wells was once previously
31	quite common. In one small village in England, bisley, all of the wells
32	and springs in the surrounding area, are decorated with thousands
33	of flowers once a year. However no part of the country compares with
34	the hills of Derbyshire, where around thirty or so villages are famous
35	for traditional well-dressing putting flower pictures beside each well
36	every summer. The incredibly strong frames supporting the pictures
37	are first soaked in a near by stream or pond (this extends the life of
38	the exhibit and then covered with a layer of clay, mixed with water and
39	salt. Full-sized drawings of the final picture, most often a religous
40	scene, are laid on the clay. The outlines are then pricked through with
41	a sharp tool. The picture is made by pushing small berrys or seeds
42	in to the clay along the lines, and filling in the colours with moss and
43	flower petals. Each of the peices overlaps the previous one, like tiles
44	on a roof, to reduce rain damage. In this way, the spectaculer flower
45	picture's last about a week, during which time everyone in the village
46	is involved in the anual fair, put on to entertain and amuse tourists.

Part 4

For questions **47–61**, read the two texts on pages **80** and **81**. Use the words in the boxes to the right of the texts to form **one** word that fits in the same numbered space in the text. Write the new word in the correct box on your answer sheet. The exercise begins with an example (**0**).

Example: | **0** | *practitioners* | **0** |

ARTICLE

Modern medicine presents a problem

Until the 20th century, most doctors were general (**0**) ..... .
Of those who (**47**) ....., the majority were (**48**) ..... – not
regarded with much respect in many countries. Experts in
other fields were found primarily on the staff of medical
schools. Progress in science brought about fundamental
changes to this situation. Modern science has made
previously (**49**) ..... developments possible. These include
the production of standardised drugs, the (**50**) ..... of the
constituents of blood and body tissues, and the use of X-
rays. The introduction of these and other (**51**) .....
techniques and practices led to a requirement for
sophisticated facilities, staffed by highly-trained doctors and
assistants. This has plainly been beneficial. However, as
treatments multiply and life (**52**) ..... rises, financing these
(**53**) ..... expensive facilities has become problematic for
governments worldwide.

(**0**)	**PRACTICE**
(**47**)	SPECIAL
(**48**)	SURGERY
(**49**)	IMAGINE
(**50**)	ANALYSE
(**51**)	REVOLUTION
(**52**)	EXPECT
(**53**)	INCREASE

EXTRACT FROM A LETTER

A special offer

On behalf of Worldwide Travel, I would like to express our **(54)** ..... gratitude to you for your ongoing **(55)** ..... to our company. Our records indicate we have made travel **(56)** ..... for you on six occasions in the last twelve months. To show how **(57)** ..... we are of your custom, we would like to offer you a very special deal. On flights to Australasia from January to March, we are making available a reduction of 20% to our most valued customers. This **(58)** ..... opportunity is unfortunately subject to seat **(59)** ..... . Visit our website for details about even greater **(60)** ..... and constantly **(61)** ..... travel information.

(54)	RESERVE
(55)	LOYAL
(56)	ARRANGE
(57)	APPRECIATE
(58)	BEAT
(59)	AVAILABLE
(60)	SAVE
(61)	DATE

Part 5

For questions **62–74**, read the following extract from a holiday brochure and use the information in it to complete the numbered gaps in the informal letter written by a woman to her friends. Write the new words in the correct boxes **on your answer sheet**. The words you need **do not occur** in the holiday brochure. **Use no more than two words for each gap.** The exercise begins with an example (**0**).

Example: | 0 | great choice | 0 |
|---|---|---|

HOLIDAY BROCHURE

Our new brochure brings you an even wider range of self-catering holidays than ever before. All the villas are located in delightful, quiet rural settings, and come fully equipped to meet most requirements. Anything else you require may be purchased in the village closest to your villa, which is always within easy walking distance. The key to your villa can be collected from the caretaker on arrival. Clean linen is provided on Mondays and Thursdays, and each villa has exclusive use of a swimming pool. The price of a hire car is included in the cost of the holiday. Our local representative will be on hand at the airport to give you assistance, if required. We offer a 50% reduction, applicable to a maximum of two children, when accompanied by two adults paying the full price. A 10% deposit secures your holiday. Early reservations are advisable to avoid disappointment.

LETTER

Dear Jayne & Martin

I've just got hold of this brochure and there's a really **(0)** ..... of holidays. The villas, which are all in the **(62)** ..... , have got nearly all the things you might **(63)** ..... a comfortable holiday. If there's anything missing you can **(64)** ..... from the local village, which can always be reached on **(65)** ..... . When you get there, you **(66)** ..... the key to your villa from the caretaker. You don't have to take sheets – clean ones are supplied **(67)** ..... weekly. You'll have a pool just **(68)** ..... – won't it be nice not having to share! You have use of a car for the week, at **(69)** ..... cost. The local representative will **(70)** ..... at the airport if you need **(71)** ..... . Another good thing is that if you take both of the children with you, as I know you will, they go for **(72)** ..... . You only have to pay 10% of the total cost to **(73)** ..... the holiday is reserved. It all sounds so good I think you should **(74)** ..... so you get what you want.

Part 6

For questions **75–80**, read the following text and then choose from the list **A–I** given below the best phrase to fill each of the spaces. Indicate your answer on the separate answer sheet. Each correct phrase may only be used once. **Some of the suggested answers do not fit at all.**

The birth of writing

Evidence of keeping records dates from around 30,000 years ago, but neither cutting notches in sticks nor the use of pictures could convey a great variety of meanings. Their capabilities were far too restricted for societies that were more and more dependent on detailed and complicated instructions. **(75)** ..... of the stage of human evolution that has become known as civilisation – life based on *civis*, the Latin word for a dweller. With its development, people were able to extend their influence over much greater areas, and to pass on knowledge from one generation to the next. **(76)** ..... largely through person-to-person contact. But once population reaches a certain level of complexity, both technological and social, personal contacts are no longer enough. Complexity demands formal, lasting and widely comprehensible written communication. The development of writing enabled people to communicate without speech. **(77)** ..... over great distances, safe in the knowledge that they did not have to rely on a messenger's memory. **(78)** ..... that could be recalled accurately years later. **(79)** ..... by populations in the future. 'History' had arrived. Once invented, the effect of writing was to stimulate the creation of yet greater social complexity. **(80)** ..... : law, commerce, administration, food production, manufacturing, education and literature.

A   Leaders could transmit instructions
B   Instructions to people have been considered necessary
C   Small communities are able to communicate
D   They could make records of objects, events and thoughts
E   Writing is one of the main distinguishing marks
F   The accumulated wisdom of civilisation would be understood
G   This had implications for every branch of society
H   Experts have achieved great success in deciphering ancient scripts
I   Systems of this kind were normally used

PAPER 4   LISTENING (approximately 45 minutes)

Part 1

You will hear a tour guide talking to a group of visitors outside an historic country house. For questions **1–8**, complete the sentences.

You will hear the recording twice.

THE HISTORY OF PARKS

The first parks appeared in the [_____ **1**] century.

In past centuries, people thought the wilder aspects of [_____ **2**] were unsafe.

Socially, parks are described as becoming an important [_____ **3**]

[_____ **4**] was considered socially significant in parks.

The fashion for parks tended to lead to the decline in importance of [_____ **5**] at country houses.

The area around a country house contained mostly [_____ **6**] rather than crops.

The only type of agriculture regularly practised in parks was [_____ **7**]

The 19th-century development of urban parks was influenced
by both rural parks and by [_____ **8**] ideas.

Part 2

You will hear the winner of a competition for young inventors talking about her invention. For questions **9–16**, complete the sentences.

Listen very carefully as you will hear the recording ONCE only.

SONIA'S INVENTION

Sonia's prize-winning invention was judged

to be [_____ **9**] as well as having commercial potential.

Sonia's invention was originally intended for

people who are [_____ **10**]

Sonia decided against a speaking thermometer

because of its [_____ **11**]

Sonia says that people in hospitals are often worried

by the attitude of [_____ **12**]

Sonia explains that her thermometer

is both [_____ **13**] and free of poisons.

Sonia needed help in the design

of the [_____ **14**] equipment in her invention.

Sonia's thermometer is powered by [_____ **15**]

Sonia describes her thermometer as

providing a [_____ **16**] immediately.

Part 3

You will hear part of an interview with a sculptor who is talking about his life and work. For questions **17–24**, complete the sentences.

You will hear the recording twice.

Alan's father originally wanted him to work

as an [   ] **17** in the family firm.

Alan describes his father as feeling

[   ] **18** when the sculpture teacher thought little of his work.

The subject that Alan eventually decided to study

at university was [   ] **19**

Alan disagreed with his father's belief that

art was not really a [   ] **20** activity.

Alan describes his father's attitude once he had

taken up sculpture as [   ] **21**

Alan describes the approach at the art college as very [   ] **22**

Harold Morton disagreed with the way

Alan was taught [   ] **23** by the college staff.

Alan accepts that the term [   ] **24** describes the type of work

he does these days.

Part 4

You will hear five short extracts in which different people are talking about living in a village. Each extract has two questions. For questions **25–34**, choose the correct answer **A**, **B** or **C**.

You will hear the recording twice.

Speaker 1

25 What does the first speaker like about living in a village?

  A the friendly people
  B the outdoor activities
  C the peaceful atmosphere

26 She would prefer a bus service which

  A the villagers would be able to organise themselves.
  B would provide daily access to the town.
  C would be used for short trips within the village.

Speaker 2

27 The second speaker thinks small local businesses are declining because

  A rural crafts are no longer in demand.
  B local property is getting too expensive.
  C the local work force is not skilled enough.

28 What does he think the villagers should do to bring more work to the area?

  A use their own savings to set up new businesses
  B wait for the state to create jobs for the unemployed
  C look for public money to supplement investment

Speaker 3

29 What does the third speaker think about shopping by computer?

    A It might prove a useful development.
    B It might be hard to adapt to it.
    C It might make an amusing change.

30 She feels the government should

    A lower petrol prices for rural areas.
    B expand the existing public transport service.
    C develop new transport systems.

Speaker 4

31 What does the fourth speaker think about working at home?

    A It's an opportunity to make new contacts.
    B It saves him the daily journey.
    C It provides him with useful leisure time.

32 Who does he think should construct the village sports facility?

    A the local council
    B the villagers themselves
    C a group of local teenagers

Speaker 5

33 What does the fifth speaker regret?

    A moving to the countryside
    B losing a source of income
    C not supporting the local amenities

34 What aspect of village life would she like to be involved in?

    A improving public transport
    B supplying necessities
    C helping with education

PAPER 5   SPEAKING (15 minutes)

There are two examiners. One (the interlocutor) conducts the test, providing you with the necessary materials and explaining what you have to do. The other examiner (the assessor) is introduced to you, but then takes no further part in the interaction.

Part 1 (3 minutes)

The interlocutor first asks you and your partner a few questions. You are then asked to find out some information about each other, on topics such as hobbies, interests, future plans, etc. You are then asked further questions by the interlocutor.

Part 2 (4 minutes)

You are each given the opportunity to talk for about a minute, and to comment briefly after your partner has spoken.

   The interlocutor gives you a set of pictures and asks you to talk about them for about one minute. It is important to listen carefully to the interlocutor's instructions. The interlocutor then asks your partner a question about your pictures and your partner responds briefly.

   You are then given another set of pictures to look at. Your partner talks about these pictures for about one minute. This time the interlocutor asks you a question about your partner's pictures and you respond briefly.

Part 3 (approximately 4 minutes)

In this part of the test you and your partner are asked to talk together. The interlocutor places a new set of pictures on the table between you. This stimulus provides the basis for a discussion. The interlocutor explains what you have to do.

Part 4 (approximately 4 minutes)

The interlocutor asks some further questions, which leads to a more general discussion of what you have talked about in Part 3. You may comment on your partner's answers if you wish.

Test 4

PAPER 1   READING (1 hour 15 minutes)

Part 1

Answer questions **1–15** by referring to the reviews of video releases from a magazine on page **93**. Indicate your answers **on the separate answer sheet**.

For questions **1–15**, answer by choosing from the reviews (**A–F**) on page 93. Some of the choices may be required more than once.

Which film

allows viewers to appreciate the director's technical skills?	**1**..........
is so entertaining that its lack of originality is unimportant?	**2**..........
has a central character whose personality reflects the setting?	**3**..........
is a greater achievement in terms of planning than of artistic merit?	**4**..........
interprets a story in a comparatively straightforward manner?	**5**..........
is criticised for its extravagant production?	**6**..........
features an actor who is sometimes good, although not really suited to his role?	**7**..........
is an older treatment of a recent cinema release?	**8**..........
is criticised for paying too much attention to appearances but too little to the plot?	**9**..........
is criticised for having a poor script?	**10**..........
features characters who care little about the harm they may be doing others?	**11**..........
is described as being rather better than many films of its type?	**12**..........
moves too slowly at the beginning?	**13**..........
has characters reminiscent of those in another director's films?	**14**..........
is described as being more faithful to its source than another film?	**15**..........

FILMS ON VIDEO

Film critic Nick James reviews some recent releases

A

Abyss

Long before *Titanic*, director James Cameron made this sweaty, claustrophobic Cold War thriller about oil riggers and navy experts trying to rescue a nuclear submarine stranded many miles beneath water. The banter and self-deprecating bravery of foreman Bud and his men rekindle memories of similarly laconic heroes in movies directed by Howard Hawks. Production design and special effects are hugely impressive. It's only the dialogue and characterisation that creak. For all the craftsmanship which goes into the film-making, the story itself is strictly B-movie material.

B

The Thin Red Line

The video release of this version of the James Jones novel about the battle for Guadalcanal directed by Andrew Marton makes a fascinating counterpart to Terrence Malick's new film. Whereas Malick's approach is mystical and poetic, Marton made a much more conventional war movie, albeit one that is often truer to the book. He concentrated on a single soldier, and on his relationship with his abrasive sergeant. Malick's film is infinitely richer and more complex, but Marton's version has its moments. The flashback sequence, in which the soldier dreams of the wife he longs for, is handled with a harshness which arguably works better than Malick's soft-focus imagery of the woman on the swing.

C

On Guard

Loosely based on Paul Féval's 1875 novel, this corny but highly watchable swashbuckler is a cut above most musketeer adventures. It has a consummate villain in Fabrice Luchini's clammy politician, orchestrating death and destruction behind the scenes. Vincent Perez makes an exuberant (if rather short-lived) hero, and while Daniel Auteuil is perhaps too moody a presence for a romp like this, he too has his moments as an acrobat-turned-swordsman. The film-makers peddle costume-drama clichés with so much wit and sparkle it never seems to matter.

D

Character

A handsome but dour tale, set in turn-of-the-century Rotterdam. The excessively detailed production and costume design leave the film looking like a museum piece. Taking his cue from the surroundings, Jan Decleir is endlessly morose as the brutal bailiff Dreverhaven, who behaves ruthlessly when evicting tenants. His antagonistic relationship with his son is at the core of the story, but the film-makers seem too busy laying on the period detail to do justice to the dark and vicious parable.

E

The Good, the Bad and the Ugly

This digitally re-mastered video re-release shows off director Leone's craftsmanship to its best advantage. The sound editing, in particular, stands out: every footstep, creaking floorboard or barking dog registers loud and clear. The storytelling is relentlessly cruel and whenever there's a lull, it only takes a burst of Morricone's magnificent music to quicken the pulse. On a moral level, there isn't much to distinguish between the good (Clint Eastwood), the bad (Lee van Cleef) and the ugly (Eli Wallach), all of whom seem equally unscrupulous as they maraud across the post-Civil War West.

F

The Longest Day

'Forty-eight international stars' trumpets the publicity for this three-hour Darryl Zanuck war epic. With four directors and 23,000 extras as well, this is one pudding which is definitely over-egged. The early sequences, in which the battle-hardened veterans wait for confirmation of when the invasion will happen, drag as much for the audience as for the soldiers. On a logistical level (if not an aesthetic one), this is an impressive enough feat but it cries out for the big screen. Panned and scanned on video, it is inevitably a diminished experience.

Part 2

For questions **16–21**, you must choose which of the paragraphs **A–G** on page **95** fit into the numbered gaps in the following magazine article. There is one extra paragraph which does not fit in any of the gaps. Indicate your answers **on the separate answer sheet**.

Where the landscape will do the walking

Despite the growth of tourism in the area, Roger Bray finds there are still undeveloped parts of Cape Cod, an exposed peninsula off the east coast of the USA

On the fragile outer shore of Cape Cod the pervading sense is of a universe in which nothing stands still. The ocean wages its war of attrition against the shifting sand, which rises from the beach into a steep cliff. Gulls wheel on the wind, swallows dart low over the water's edge.

16

The simple reason is that, here, more than in most places, to get off the roads and away from the most easily accessible beaches is to experience the Cape not just as a holiday retreat for urban Americans but as it has always been.

17

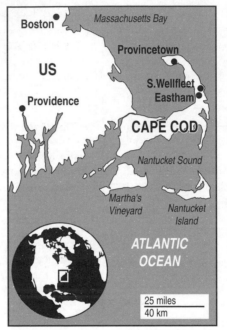

This is mainly because a large swathe of it was established in 1961 as a national park. Our search for recommended hikes took us to the internet – but the maps were hard to follow. We tried bookshops but to no avail. There were books listing walks, to be sure, but the routes they covered were much too short.

18

Following its directions made for superb hiking. To cover the whole of the route we wanted to do would have involved linear sections totalling about 50 kilometres. There were circular itineraries, however, varying in length between about 12 and 20 kilometres, though slow going on soft sand makes them seem longer.

19

One route took us along the Old King's Highway, once a stagecoach route, into the middle of an eerie swamp of Atlantic white cedar, where the sunlight streamed between shaggy barked trunks and where the park management has built a boardwalk and provided nature information.

20

The circuit concluded with an intoxicating hike along the beach. To our right rose the huge sandy cliff, threatening to slide and bury the unwary. Henry Beston, in *The Outermost House*, his lyrical account of a year spent here in the 1920s, describes how, after the cliff was pushed back 6 metres or so by a momentous storm, the long buried wreckage of ships emerged from it, as fruit from a sliced pudding.

21

The shingled Whalewalk Inn was also a delight. It lies behind a white painted picket fence on a leafy road on the fringe of Eastham. It was built in 1830 by Henry Harding, a whaling captain when that industry was at its peak. Later it was used as a farmhouse and a salt works. Nowadays, people also find it a relaxing place to stay.

A It continued to the South Wellfleet sea cliff where Marconi broadcast the first transatlantic wireless message in 1903, sending greetings in Morse code from President Theodore Roosevelt to King Edward VII. The transmitting station was scrapped in 1920 but a model recalls how it looked, its antennae suspended between tall timber masts.

B If we had sauntered a few kilometres from the car park to stand for a while on that great beach, we might still have felt the whirling of the universe. But without a day of serious hiking to sharpen our appetites, would we have appreciated the food so much?

C On the other side, however, there was nothing but ocean, jade green inshore, ink blue farther out, between us and the coast of north-west Spain. Although this was a week of near flawless weather in May, we were lucky to encounter only a handful of other walkers. In high summer, when the roads are clogged and there are queues for restaurant tables, it is harder to find an empty stretch of beach.

D Because, for all the impact of tourism, which nearly triples the population in summer, there are still lonely parts of this storm-scoured, glacial peninsula which have changed little during the last 150 years.

E We tried several of them. Sometimes we were on woodland trails shaded partly by pitch pine and black oak, sometimes on high windy cliffs overlooking the sea, and sometimes on the foreshore, where we were made diminutive by the huge sky and curving beach of white gold sand.

F Henry David Thoreau wrote that 'even the sedentary man here enjoys a breadth of view which is almost equivalent to motion'. Perhaps that was why it proved so difficult to find a guide for long hikes. People must wonder why they need to expend effort when they can let the landscape do the walking.

G Staff at the inquiry desk of the Cape Cod National Seashore's Salt Pond visitor centre were no help, either. But in the centre's bookshop, we struck gold at last. Adam Gamble's *In the Footsteps of Thoreau*, published locally two years ago, has a section tracing the writer's progress in 1849 from Eastham to Race Point Beach, where he turned towards Provincetown, the Cape's outermost community, now a gathering place for whale watchers.

Part 3

Read the following magazine article and then answer questions **22–28** on page **98**. **On your answer sheet**, indicate the letter **A**, **B**, **C** or **D** against the number of each question, **22–28**. Give only one answer to each question.

Under Sarah's Spell

Sarah Janson is a *trompe-l'oeil* artist whose paintings are designed to deceive the eye by creating the illusion of reality. Here she is interviewed by Joanna Watt

There cannot be many artists who do not sign their work unless they are asked to. Sarah Janson, a *trompe-l'oeil* artist, is one. She is not remotely interested in the concept of the artist as creator, let alone that of the artist as genius: 'It's not the artist who is important, but the work,' she states. Janson is so self-deprecating that she would almost like you to believe that her trompe-l'oeil works paint themselves.

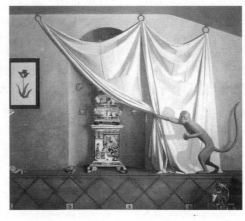

All of which does not bode well for a magazine interview. 'I just don't like to shout about myself,' she says, and then covers her face in horror when asked if she minds being photographed for the feature. Cut to her sitting room 30 minutes later (a wonderful space in a block of artists' studios in London, filled with paintings and drawings) and you find two women bent double with hysteria. Her confidence gained, the interview becomes a fascinating, amusing (and sometimes hilarious) encounter.

Janson has been a trompe-l'oeil artist for sixteen years, after two years' solid drawing at art school ('the best training any artist can ever have'), a degree in graphic illustration and a stint at a publishing house. But illustration never really satisfied her, and she joined a specialist decorator, Jim Smart ('one of the best in his day'). Smart asked her to do one trompe-l'oeil, and that was it. 'Suddenly my interest got channelled,' she says. She left to set up on her own, 'not really knowing where I was going, but feeling that I was on the road to somewhere.' Her instinct was right.

Janson's observational skills and fascination with detail (gained through illustrating) proved essential qualities for a trompe-l'oeil artist. 'People often ask me where they can learn trompe-l'oeil. But no one can teach you. Trompe-l'oeil is the school of life. It's all about observation.' She insists (in that self-deprecating way) that she is still learning. 'The moment you think that you've mastered a field you might as well give up.' She is also brutally honest about her 'failings' ('I can't paint bread; it always looks like grey concrete') and is frank about her mathematical abilities. Faced with a huge commission for the domed chapel ceiling at Lulworth Castle, she became totally confused when calculating measurements. 'I thought to myself, "You're not Michelangelo. Who do you think you are?"' This habit of self-questioning and a reluctance to openly acknowledge her skill has spawned an oddly distanced attitude to her talent. Janson often speaks in the third person: 'When I finished that ceiling, I thought, "Well *I* didn't do it, *she* did".'

Of course, her trompe-l'oeil schemes can speak for themselves. Janson's work is in a league of its own, far above those who have jumped on the bandwagon (the art of trompe-l'oeil has experienced something of a revival, but not with entirely satisfactory results) and she has a string of major corporate and private commissions behind her. Much of her work is inspired by architecture or made for architectural settings. There is the trompe-l'oeil dining room for one client, based on the façade of a Venetian palazzo, and the painting at the end of a corridor in a flat, which gives the illusion that you can step into two further rooms.

There is always a danger with trompe-l'oeil, though, that once you get the joke, your attention is lost, something of which Janson is acutely aware. 'Trompe-l'oeil has to do two things. First, it must draw you in; it's got to trick you. Secondly, it has to hold you and then engage your imagination. That is the most important part.'

While trompe-l'oeil has to be clever, it must also, Janson believes, be personal to the client. 'I love the interaction with clients; that is where the ideas are born,' she says. 'Without the rapport, the job of creating a trompe-l'oeil scheme becomes rather difficult. Some clients have firm ideas about what they want; others do not. You have to be willing to listen. You have to get inside a client's imagination.' Many have become friends, not least because Janson practically lives with them if she works on site.

Janson is generous in praise of her clients. 'I am very grateful for the mad ones who have let me loose on their walls,' she confesses. And, they too, seem delighted with her, which is why she is constantly busy – despite her inclination to play down her talent. 'I really don't like to shout about myself,' she repeats at the end. 'Like my work, I am very restrained. I don't want it to shout. You become bored with things that shout.' True, perhaps, but you could never really become bored with Janson or her work. It certainly deserves to become better known, and I am prepared to incur her wrath while I blow her trumpet.

22 After spending time with Janson, the interviewer concludes that

 A Janson has little faith in journalists.
 B Janson dislikes interviews in her home.
 C her initial doubts about Janson were wrong.
 D her first questions to Janson were threatening.

23 What motivated Janson to start her own business as a trompe-l'oeil artist?

 A It was something she was well qualified to do.
 B She was unhappy with her previous employer.
 C She was convinced it was what she wanted to do.
 D It was something that would help her achieve her ambitions.

24 What advice does Janson give to people interested in becoming trompe-l'oeil artists?

 A It would be a mistake to become over-confident.
 B Practice is the only way to improve shortcomings.
 C Experience in different art forms helps develop essential skills.
 D A lot can be gained from looking at the work of other artists.

25 What point does the interviewer make about Janson's work in paragraph five?

 A It is of an exceptional quality.
 B Some people regard it as strange.
 C It is better suited to small locations.
 D Janson regrets some of the commissions she has taken on.

26 What does Janson say about trompe-l'oeil as an art form?

 A It has limited commercial appeal.
 B The most successful pieces avoid humour.
 C A small number of people accept it as genuine art.
 D The difficulty lies in sustaining people's interest.

27 What does Janson say about her clients?

 A She prefers to work with clients who have a lot of imagination.
 B Some clients have ideas which are less practical than others.
 C She is reluctant to take on commissions if she cannot agree with the client.
 D A commission is easier if you can discover what kind of ideas the client has.

28 What does the interviewer say in the last paragraph?

 A She is puzzled by the way Janson describes her clients.
 B She realises that Janson may not like what she has written about her.
 C She is sure that certain types of art soon lose their appeal.
 D She feels that trompe-l'oeil is unlikely to become a more popular art form.

Part 4

Answer questions **29–45** by referring to the magazine article about writers on page **100**. Indicate your answers **on the separate answer sheet**.

For questions **29–45**, choose your answers from the writers (**A–E**). Some of the choices may be required more than once.

Which writer

says that he is not the kind of writer who wants a solitary existence?	29..........
avoids showing his work to anyone before it has been thoroughly revised?	30..........
thinks that some people may have the wrong impression of a writer's life?	31..........
no longer feels uneasy about the kind of life writing involves?	32..........
points out how much revision can be involved in writing a novel?	33..........
says that on some days he knows in advance that writing will be difficult?	34..........
says that he has a limited amount of inspiration?	35..........
says that It Is essential, for a writer's sanity, to spend some time in the company of others?	36..........
admits that he does not actually work for the whole time he spends at his desk?	37..........
says that he finds it difficult to assess his own writing in a critical way?	38..........
forces himself to get something written when he is having difficulties?	39..........
thinks that he writes better when working at a fast pace?	40..........
draws a contrast between days when it is easy to write and those when it is not?	41..........
requires little persuasion to reward himself for work he has done?	42..........
says that he feels comfortable with the kind of writing day that he has established for himself?	43..........
does not look forward to reading published opinions of his work?	44..........
always tries to delay the time when he has to start writing?	45..........

A Writer's Day

We interviewed five contemporary male novelists to find out how they approach their writing and how they typically spend their day

A

I'm no good at mixed days – it's either work or play. If it's a work day, then I'll start with a huge mug of strong black coffee and then I'll go to my study at the top of the house. It's completely lined with books and has a 'Do Not Disturb' sign on the door.

I've learned to start writing early and to have a scene hanging over from the day before. I'm obsessive about silence. I can't talk in the middle of work – if I talk, the morning is over. Momentum is important to my novels – if I'm too leisurely, I can feel the tension fading away. Dialogue is the best – blissfully easy, like hearing voices in your head and taking dictation. A few years ago, I was writing 5,000 words a day – now, though, it's only half that.

When I go out, I do all the things you're supposed to as a writer, like going out to London clubs. But when people see you at book launches they forget that being a writer is also about that little thing in between – sitting on your own all day. But you've got to have contact with the outside world and real people or you can go completely mad.

B

I'm completely envious of people who write in the mornings and do what they like in the afternoon. I work through the day and treat writing like an office job. If it's not going well, I keep pushing at it and get it sorted out. I don't get a lot of ideas. I tend to get just one and then run with it. Towards the end of a book, when I think I've got to get an idea for the next one, I start to feel panicky. But something always comes along.

My office is in a flat about ten minutes from our house. It's good to have a geographical break between home and work. I arrive about 9 am, have a coffee and then I'll just get on with it and work through until lunchtime. There's a definite post-lunch dip – that's when I have another coffee. But in the end, the only way I get concentration back is by pushing it.

My wife picks me up about 6.30 and we go home together. I've been doing this for ten years now. It's a routine that suits me and, to be honest, I'm always a little worried about breaking it.

C

My seven-month-old daughter, Matilda, gets me up around 6.30 and I'll play with her for a couple of hours, then go to my desk. I officially sit there for three hours, but I'll do an hour's work.

Like a lot of writers, I tend to get a great sense of achievement very easily. One good sentence entitles me to half an hour off – two or three lines means I can watch daytime TV. My study is at one end of the flat and my wife and daughter are at the other. In theory, no congress takes place until lunchtime, but actually we pop in and out all the time. I've never been one of those writers who likes being isolated – I want people around me all the time. At the moment, I'm plotting my next novel and am in a dreamy state. It's hard to convince people that I'm actually working, but this is a crucial part of the process.

A book takes me about three years in all. I always start out very slowly and then gather speed towards the end. I don't think this is a good way to write at all.

D

I have a really slow start to the day. I'll do anything to put off starting work. I have toast, read newspapers – I have to do the crossword every morning – and deal with my post. I write quite slowly and not in chronological order. I've structured the story before I start, so I can hop around, which I think keeps my writing fresh. Sometimes I wake up and just know it's not going to work – because I'm just not in the right mood – but I know that it's only temporary. Once you've got the first draft down, you know that it's going to be OK. It's awful having to relinquish it to my editor, but I'm curious to know what other people think. I find it impossible to be objective about my own words.

When I started writing and just stayed at home I felt incredibly guilty but now it feels normal. Lots of my friends are creative and don't go to offices, which helps. When we go out we don't talk about work – we gossip about the people we know instead. But if I want to use anything my friends have told me, I always ask.

E

I start writing at about 10.30 am. I don't open any mail before that so I haven't got anything on my mind and the desk is clear. I write until 1.30 pm. Sometimes getting the words out is like pulling teeth – other days it all spills out freely.

Someone once said that there was no such thing as writing, only re-writing. For my first book, I did no less than 12 drafts. With the first draft of a book, I just try to capture the energy and try to get something down which I can work with. I would die of embarrassment if anyone saw it.

At lunchtime I like to get out of the flat. It's odd going into the outside world – you feel as if you're in a light trance. But after a ten-minute walk in the drizzle I'm usually all right. I spend 90 per cent of my time on my own. My contact with the outside world generally happens in great bursts, when I go abroad to publicise my books.

I've just finished my third novel and it's a nerve-racking time. I really dread being at the mercy of book reviewers. But when it comes down to it, I know what my book is like – I don't need to be told by other people.

PAPER 2   WRITING (2 hours)

Part 1

1   Your college contributed a lot of money to support the building of a new Arts Centre. In return, the Arts Centre promised to provide a number of things which would be of advantage to your college.

Your college principal asked you to attend the opening of the Arts Centre. At the opening you were impressed by many of the things that you saw, but you were disappointed that the Centre did not seem to have kept all its promises to the college.

Read the memo from your principal below and, on page **102**, the handout about the Arts Centre, which you picked up at the opening and on which you have made some notes. Then, **using the information appropriately**, write a letter to the Arts Centre manager, thanking him for the invitation to the opening, commenting on what you liked about the Centre and explaining why you were disappointed about the promises that have not been kept. In your letter, you should also suggest a meeting to discuss some of the issues further.

MEMO

To: **Secretary of Student Committee**
From: **Principal**

Re: **Opening of new Arts Centre**

Unfortunately, I am too busy to attend the opening of the new Arts Centre and, as you are the secretary of the Student Committee, I think it would be appropriate for you to go in my place.

As you know, our college contributed a lot of money to help build the Centre and in return they promised us:

- free use of recording studio, music and rehearsal rooms
- use of theatre for annual student productions in December and May
- a programme of unusual, international films to fit in with our cinema courses
- use of Arts Library
- 10% student discount on all tickets.

After the opening, please could you write to the Manager of the Arts Centre, and thank him for the invitation? If any of their promises have not been kept, you will need to explain in your letter why these things are important to the college and arrange a meeting to discuss the issues.

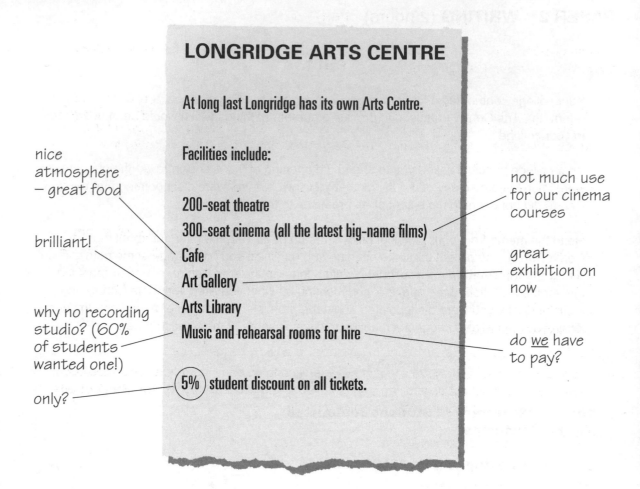

LONGRIDGE ARTS CENTRE

At long last Longridge has its own Arts Centre.

Facilities include:

200-seat theatre
300-seat cinema (all the latest big-name films)
Cafe
Art Gallery
Arts Library
Music and rehearsal rooms for hire

5% student discount on all tickets.

nice atmosphere – great food

brilliant!

why no recording studio? (60% of students wanted one!)

only?

not much use for our cinema courses

great exhibition on now

do we have to pay?

Now write your **letter** to the newspaper editor, as outlined on page **101** (approximately 250 words). You do not need to include postal addresses. You should use your own words as far as possible.

Part 2

Choose **one** of the following writing tasks. Your answer should follow exactly the instructions given. Write approximately 250 words.

2   A technology magazine, *International Technology Today*, has asked its readers to submit articles on the impact of mobile phones on modern society. In your article, you should discuss the different personal and business uses of mobile phones and assess the advantages and disadvantages of this technology.

Write your **article**.

3   Your town is hoping to host a sports event next year, which will attract competitors from other countries. The organisers of this sports event need to ensure that the chosen venue has an adequate range of facilities for visitors. Write a proposal to the organising committee to persuade them that your town is a suitable venue. Your proposal should include information on accommodation, transport and entertainment.

Write your **proposal**.

4   You have been asked to write a leaflet giving advice to students from other countries about how to get the most out of studying in your college. The title is ***Studying and Student Life*** and the leaflet must include advice relating to:
   • methods of study
   • suitable types of accommodation
   • social life.

Write the **text for the leaflet**.

5   You recently visited a trade fair in an English-speaking country and you feel it would be good for your company to have a stand at this fair next year. The head of the marketing department has asked you to write a report, describing what you saw and experienced at the trade fair this year and explaining why your company would benefit from having a stand there next year.

Write your **report**.

PAPER 3 ENGLISH IN USE (1 hour 30 minutes)

Part 1

For questions **1–15**, read the article below and then decide which answer on page **105** best fits each space. Indicate your answer **on the separate answer sheet**. The exercise begins with an example **(0)**.

Example: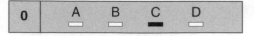

We really can tell if we are being watched

Stories about how people somehow know when they are being watched have been going around for years. However, few **(0)** ..... have been made to investigate the phenomenon scientifically. Now, with the completion of the largest ever study of the so-called *staring effect*, there is impressive evidence that this is a recognisable and **(1)** ..... sixth sense. The study **(2)** ..... hundreds of children. For the experiments, they sat with their eyes **(3)** ..... so they could not see, and with their backs to other children, who were told to either stare at them or look away. Time and time again the results showed that the children who could not see were able to **(4)** ..... when they were being stared at. In a **(5)** ..... of more than 18,000 trials **(6)** ..... worldwide, the children **(7)** ..... sensed when they were being watched almost 70% of the time. The experiment was repeated with the **(8)** ..... precaution of putting the children who were being watched outside the room, **(9)** ..... from the starers by the windows. This was done just in case there was some **(10)** ..... going on with the children telling each other whether they were looking or not. This **(11)** ..... the possibility of sounds being **(12)** ..... between the children. The results, though less impressive, were more or less the same. Dr Sheldrake, the biologist who designed the study, believes that the results are **(13)** ..... enough to find out through further experiments **(14)** ..... how the staring effect might actually **(15)** ..... .

0	**A**	tries	**B**	tests	**(C)**	attempts	**D**	aims
1	**A**	genuine	**B**	accepted	**C**	received	**D**	sure
2	**A**	involved	**B**	contained	**C**	comprised	**D**	enclosed
3	**A**	shaded	**B**	wrapped	**C**	masked	**D**	covered
4	**A**	find	**B**	notice	**C**	tell	**D**	reveal
5	**A**	sum	**B**	collection	**C**	mass	**D**	total
6	**A**	worked over	**B**	worked through	**C**	carried on	**D**	carried out
7	**A**	correctly	**B**	exactly	**C**	thoroughly	**D**	perfectly
8	**A**	attached	**B**	added	**C**	connected	**D**	increased
9	**A**	separated	**B**	parted	**C**	split	**D**	divided
10	**A**	pretending	**B**	lying	**C**	cheating	**D**	deceiving
11	**A**	prevented	**B**	omitted	**C**	evaded	**D**	ended
12	**A**	delivered	**B**	transported	**C**	transmitted	**D**	distributed
13	**A**	satisfying	**B**	convincing	**C**	concluding	**D**	persuading
14	**A**	really	**B**	carefully	**C**	definitely	**D**	precisely
15	**A**	come about	**B**	be looked at	**C**	set out	**D**	be held up

Part 2

For questions **16–30**, complete the following article by writing each missing word in the correct box on your answer sheet. **Use only one word for each space**. The exercise begins with an example **(0)**.

Example:

0	*since*	0
		<u>– –</u>

The toughest runners

These runners are the ones who have completed every London Marathon **(0)** ..... the first race in 1981. They are the toughest runners of **(16)** ..... . These athletes, **(17)** ..... honour of both their mental and physical strength, have been given a permanent entry in the event for the rest of their lives, provided that they do not miss a year. Other people have run the race faster or under greater handicaps, **(18)** ..... these are athletes with a mission. For **(19)** ..... , the annual event is a way of life, not just a worthy fund-raising exercise **(20)** ..... a single challenge. Bill O'Connor is one of these runners. In **(21)** ..... case, running is a daily ritual which began in New Zealand **(22)** ..... , as a youngster, he pounded along the wet sand on the edge of the Tasman Sea. Now aged fifty, **(23)** ..... working as a mathematics teacher at a school in London, he retains his fascination **(24)** ..... the London Marathon and the activity of running. He says, 'When the first London Marathon was held, I thought **(25)** ..... myself that here was a challenge. I thought that if **(26)** ..... was only going to be one race, I wanted to have run in **(27)** ..... .' But the London Marathon became the most impressive success story in British sport and Bill O'Connor has been a constant part of it. **(28)** ..... he ever felt that he would fail to finish? 'In 1985. It was a beautiful day and I started running much **(29)** ..... fast for the first mile and got worried. So I slowed down for the next mile. Yet **(30)** ..... I expected I would take at least four hours, I finished in two hours thirty-four minutes and twenty-nine seconds.' It is his best time so far.

Part 3

In **most** lines of the following text, there is **either** a spelling **or** a punctuation error. For each numbered line **31–46**, write the correctly spelt word or show the correct punctuation in the box on your answer sheet. **Some lines are correct.** Indicate these lines with a tick (✓) in the box. The exercise begins with three examples (**0**), (**00**) and (**000**).

Examples:	0	astronomical	0
	00	✓	00
	000	night, the	000

Solar eclipse

0 Most astronomicall events that influence the Earth, apart from the

00 occasional asteroid impact, do so in a regular fashion, such as day and

000 night the tides and the seasons. There is, however, one event that has

31 a tremendous impact on the Earth that of the total eclipse. For a few

32 minutes, broad daylight changes, to complete darkness as the Moon

33 totally hides the Sun. This darkness is acompanied by many spectacular

34 effects, and it also provides a rare opportunity for phisicists to make

35 observations' that are impossible at any other time. However, as a total

36 solar eclipse is a sudden interuption of the day, it can also have an effect

37 on plants and animals that are used to the regular cycle of day and night.

38 As total eclipses occur on average once every 360-years at any particular

39 location, there is little chance of any living thing becoming accustomed to

40 them. In fact, there are some amazing stories of the unusual behavour of

41 animals as a total eclipse approaches. In australia, for example, one

42 observer said, I found myself having to calm a distressed parrot, which

43 fell to the ground a moment or so before the total eclipse' Joanna Kale,

44 another observer, found her head surrounded by a cloud of insects that

45 dispersed when the Sun finally emmerged from the eclipse. So, as these

46 examples show, the Suns presence has an astonishing influence on life on Earth.

Part 4

For questions **47–61**, read the two texts on pages **108** and **109**. Use the words in the boxes to the right of the texts to form **one** word that fits in the same numbered space in the text. Write the new word in the correct box on your answer sheet. The exercise begins with an example (**0**).

Example:

0	*recommendation*	0

REVIEW

Hamlet

If you are planning to go to the cinema this weekend, my **(0)** ….. would be to go and see this highly-acclaimed version of Hamlet. This is the first time the full Shakespeare text has been brought to the big screen. At no point is it **(47)** ….. , despite being four hours long. This ambitious **(48)** ….. is noteworthy because of the **(49)** ….. of its sets and the **(50)** ….. performances. It is interesting to see the portrayal of Claudius as a **(51)** ….. man, and Kate Winslet makes a particularly powerful Ophelia. Kenneth Branagh, as Hamlet, brings to life the **(52)** ….. of the character.

It is a visual triumph which brings together an impressive international cast and makes optimum use of its beautiful location. This certainly is a truly **(53)** ….. film.

(0)	**RECOMMEND**
(47)	MONOTONY
(48)	ADAPT
(49)	ELEGANT
(50)	EXCEL
(51)	SYMPATHY
(52)	COMPLEX
(53)	REMARK

JOB ADVERTISEMENT

Museum Manager

The Petrie Museum of **(54)** ….. material from Ancient Egypt is of international **(55)** ….. . Recently voted one of London's top ten little-known museums, it deserves much wider **(56)** ….. . We are looking for a Museum Manager to take charge of the day-to-day running of the museum. This new post combines both a practical and a strategic role. **(57)** ….. will include taking a lead on the **(58)** ….. of the museum's documentation, and devising programmes to increase the **(59)** ….. of the museum.

The new manager will oversee the long overdue redecoration of the building, make several new staff **(60)** ….. and supervise **(61)** ….. courses.

(54) ARCHAEOLOGY

(55) SIGNIFY

(56) RECOGNISE

(57) RESPONSIBLE

(58) COMPUTER

(59) ACCESSIBLE

(60) APPOINT

(61) EDUCATE

Part 5

For questions **62–74**, read the following notes written by a student who went to see the end-of-term show at her college. Use the information in it to complete the numbered gaps in the review she wrote for the college magazine. Write the new words in the correct boxes **on your answer sheet**. The words you need **do not occur** in the informal notes. **Use no more than two words for each gap.** The exercise begins with an example (**0**).

Example:

0	*very impressed*	0

NOTES

COLLEGE SUMMER SHOW

Absolutely great! Really high standard – nothing amateur about this!
NB Stage done so it could be speedily moved around for different bits of the show.

1. **Jazz band** – a really lively 30-minute programme featuring Janette Maclaine, who sang a nice choice of well-known songs (everyone thought the same – she was the star of the show).

2. **Drama society** – short play by David Owen (who will be graduating at the end of term) about some of the major problems in today's world. A bit gloomy, but all the students in the cast played their parts really well and it did make me think.

3. **Mini-plays** – short and had everyone in fits of laughter.

4. **Close** – all the performers on stage, everyone sang and danced – brought everyone in the audience to their feet shouting for more.

All in all, this was an evening no one will forget.

COLLEGE MAGAZINE REVIEW

THE SUMMER SHOW

I was **(0)** ..... by the high standard of this year's summer show – it was good enough to have been a **(62)** ..... performance. The stage had been **(63)** ..... to allow for good continuity between the different parts of the show.

To **(64)** ..... , a jazz band entertained the audience with a really lively half-hour performance, including a lovely **(65)** ..... of popular songs. Everyone was in total **(66)** ..... that Janette Maclaine was the star of the show.

Next, the drama society performed a short play written by David Owen, a student in **(67)** ..... year at the college. The play addressed some of the most **(68)** ..... issues in contemporary society. I found it **(69)** ..... depressing, but the **(70)** ..... was superb and it was thought-provoking.

The series of plays that followed didn't **(71)** ..... and they were such a contrast – everyone in the audience found them very **(72)** ..... .

The evening ended with a song and dance routine that brought the **(73)** ..... audience to their feet.

An occasion that will **(74)** ..... for a long time!

Part 6

For questions **75–80**, read the following text and then choose from the list **A–I** given below the best phrase to fill each of the spaces. Indicate your answers on the separate answer sheet. Each correct phrase may only be used once. **Some of the suggested answers do not fit at all.**

Ancient forests

Hundreds of years ago, British forests were areas of countryside used for hunting – sources of deer skins and meat. A typical example was the New Forest in the south of England, which was claimed and enclosed by King William I in about 1079. In this way, many large areas of forests were taken by the King for his own personal use. The importance of these royal hunting forests to the economy of the times is shown by the restrictions **(75)** ..... . With more and more land being cleared for agriculture, farming was almost brought to a halt in the enclosed forest areas, the aim being to preserve the trees **(76)** ..... . The King's deer were protected by strict penalties for illegal hunting and, perhaps most important of all, local farmers were not allowed to build fences **(77)** ..... . The difficulties that this caused were recognised, however, and farmers were granted rights **(78)** ..... . By the 15th century, the use of wood, the principal raw material of the age, had so increased that concern arose over supplies for building and fuel **(79)** ..... . As a result, the next step in enclosing land was for tree planting. This grew swiftly in importance as a source of income for the King. These enclosures had the effect of reducing still further the land available to ordinary people for feeding animals, **(80)** ..... . These problems continued until the late 19th century, when new laws were passed to prevent further enclosure of land.

A   which were no longer sufficient to meet the demand
B   which therefore changed considerably over the centuries
C   which supplied food for the deer and sheltered them beneath their branches
D   which might prevent animals from moving freely
E   which was consequently ideal for animal farming
F   which led to even more disputes than the earlier ban on building fences
G   which were placed on those unlucky enough to live there
H   which allowed them to feed their livestock for limited periods in the open forest
I   which were their principal source of warmth and food

Visual materials for the Speaking test

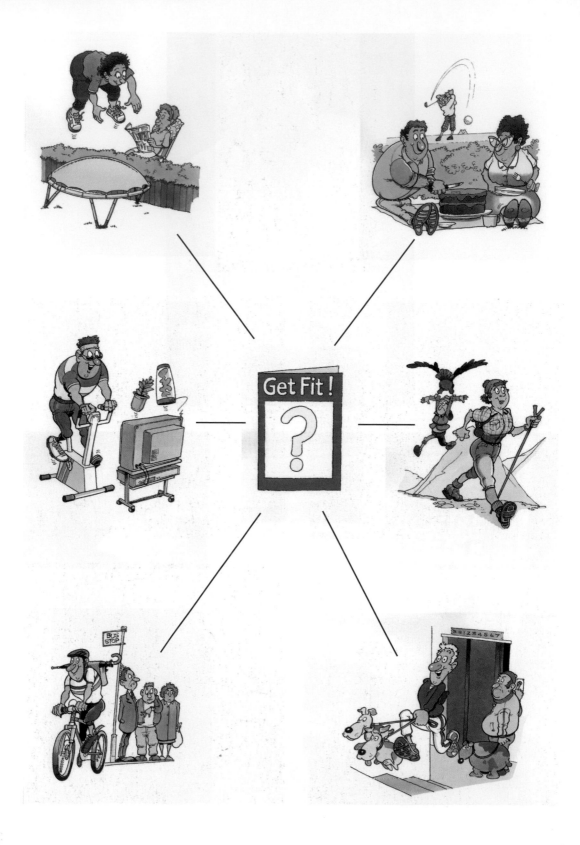

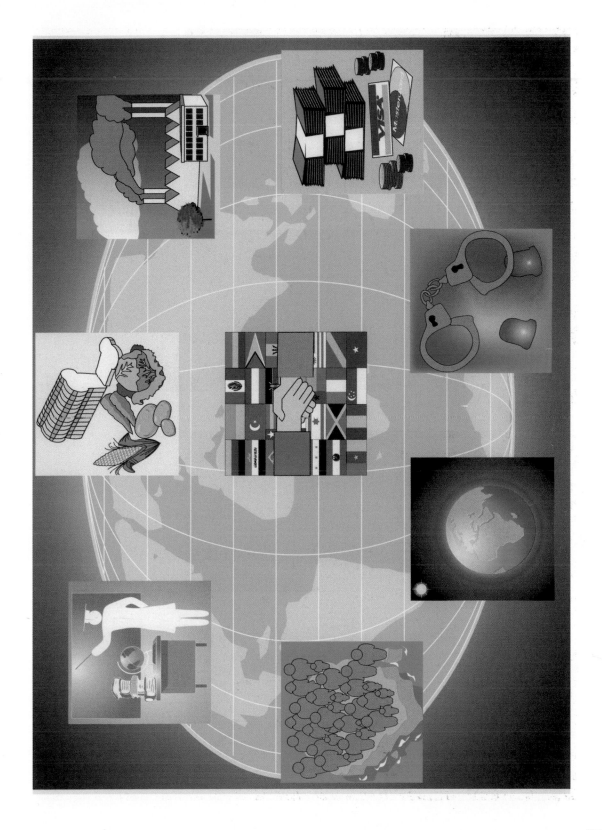

PAPER 4   LISTENING (approximately 45 minutes)

Part 1

You will hear a journalist called Peter Smith talking about a trip he made to the Arctic seas around the North Pole. For questions **1–8**, complete the sentences.

You will hear the recording twice.

ARCTIC TRIP

After reading a book called

| | **1** | , Peter decided to sail to the North Pole.

Peter says that when sailing in this part of the world, you feel as if you are

| | **2** |

Peter says it is essential to have the necessary

| | **3** | on board to deal with problems.

In summer, the temperature of the water always remains

| | **4** | at the surface.

It is necessary to have | | **5** | in the cabin.

The crew couldn't explain why there were | | **6** | in the sea.

Peter was disappointed not to see any | | **7** | during the trip.

People usually visit the area as part of

| | **8** | and see very few places.

Part 2

You will hear the headteacher of a school talking to a group of parents about an international student exchange programme. For questions **9–16**, complete the sentences.

Listen very carefully as you will hear the recording ONCE only.

INTERNATIONAL EXCHANGE PROGRAMME

The school's exchange programme is called _____ **9**

Children first get to know their exchange partners by taking part in a _____ **10** scheme.

The programme is not only intended for students who enjoy using _____ **11**

The two countries most often visited on the programme are _____ *and* _____ **12**

Some students suffer from problems such as homesickness and _____ **13**

To help students who have problems, a qualified _____ **14** is always available.

Local visits are described as being _____ **15** and also educationally valuable.

Students enjoy visiting _____ **16** parks most of all.

Part 3

You will hear part of an interview with Norman Cowley, a well-known novelist and biographer. For questions **17–23**, choose the correct answer **A**, **B**, **C** or **D**.

You will hear the recording twice.

17 How does Norman Cowley feel about his first novel?

    A proud of the directness of the writing
    B pleased by the way the characters interacted
    C worried by the over-refined style he used then
    D sad that he could never write anything like it again

18 What was Norman Cowley's reaction to one very bad review of his second novel?

    A He was surprised as he thought this book was well written.
    B He thought the detailed criticisms of the book were unjustified.
    C He thought the review was written in a clever and amusing style.
    D He did not regard the critic as well qualified to judge his work.

19 What value does Norman Cowley see in book reviews now?

    A They encourage writers to try new subjects.
    B They motivate less committed writers.
    C They give young writers long-term guidance.
    D They are part of a necessary selection process.

20 Norman Cowley thinks that if a writer uses people he knows well in a book,

    A those characters will be very realistic.
    B it will become rather tedious to write.
    C readers will find the dialogue very natural.
    D the writer will have to alter them in some way.

21 Norman Cowley believes that some modern novels

    A are much too violent.
    B contain too much fantasy.
    C don't analyse the characters sufficiently.
    D don't describe the setting adequately.

22 What does Norman Cowley see as the main thing a novel should give the reader?

    A psychological theories
    B a new angle on life
    C a thrilling story
    D beautiful language

23 What does Norman Cowley like about writing a biography?

    A basing a narrative on actual events
    B getting to know a famous person very well
    C deciding how to describe a complex personality
    D making the subject known to a wider audience

Part 4

You will hear five short extracts in which different people are talking about the means of escape they use to cope with the demands of their working lives.

You will hear the recording twice. While you listen you must complete both tasks.

TASK ONE

For questions **24–28**, match the extracts with what each speaker finds demanding about their work, listed **A–H**.

A	emotional involvement	
B	an excess of information	Speaker 1 **24**
C	clashes of personality	Speaker 2 **25**
D	everyday problems	Speaker 3 **26**
E	arguments about procedures	
F	extended working hours	Speaker 4 **27**
G	being in the public eye	Speaker 5 **28**
H	lack of physical space	

TASK TWO

For questions **29–33**, match the extracts with what attracts the speakers to their different means of escape, listed **A–H**.

A	the feeling of being artistic	
B	the warmth of the relationships	Speaker 1 **29**
C	the fulfilment of a childhood ambition	Speaker 2 **30**
D	the idea of taking a risk	Speaker 3 **31**
E	the chance to overindulge yourself	
F	the change of activities	Speaker 4 **32**
G	the luxury provided	Speaker 5 **33**
H	the spirit of co-operation	

PAPER 5   SPEAKING (15 minutes)

There are two examiners. One (the interlocutor) conducts the test, providing you with the necessary materials and explaining what you have to do. The other examiner (the assessor) is introduced to you, but then takes no further part in the interaction.

Part 1 (3 minutes)

The interlocutor first asks you and your partner a few questions. You are then asked to find out some information about each other, on topics such as hobbies, interests, future plans, etc. You are then asked further questions by the interlocutor.

Part 2 (4 minutes)

You are each given the opportunity to talk for about a minute, and to comment briefly after your partner has spoken.

The interlocutor gives you a set of pictures and asks you to talk about them for about one minute. It is important to listen carefully to the interlocutor's instructions. The interlocutor then asks your partner a question about your pictures and your partner responds briefly.

You are then given another set of pictures to look at. Your partner talks about these pictures for about one minute. This time the interlocutor asks you a question about your partner's pictures and you respond briefly.

Part 3 (approximately 4 minutes)

In this part of the test you and your partner are asked to talk together. The interlocutor places a new set of pictures on the table between you. This stimulus provides the basis for a discussion. The interlocutor explains what you have to do.

Part 4 (approximately 4 minutes)

The interlocutor asks some further questions, which leads to a more general discussion of what you have talked about in Part 3. You may comment on your partner's answers if you wish.

Paper 5 frames

Test 1

Note: In the live test, there will be both an assessor and an interlocutor in the room.

The visual material for **Test 1** appears on pages C1, C4 (Part 2), and C2–3 (Part 3).

Part 1   (3 minutes)

Interlocutor: Good morning (afternoon/evening). My name is ...... and this is my colleague, ...

And your names are ...... ?

Can I have your mark sheets, please?

Thank you.

First of all, we'd like to know a little about you.

(Select one or two questions and ask candidates in turn, as appropriate.)

- Where do you both/all live?
- How long have you been studying English?
- Have you been studying English together?
- What countries have you visited?

Now I'd like you to ask **each other** something about

(Select one or two prompts in any order, as appropriate.)

- things you particularly like about living in this country.
- entertainment and leisure facilities in this area.
- your reasons for studying English.
- a change you would like to make to your life in the future.

(Ask candidates one or more further questions in any order, as appropriate.)

- How important do you think English is in this country?
- How would you feel about going to live abroad permanently?
- What interesting events have happened in your life recently?
- Who do you think has had the greatest influence on your life so far? (Why?)
- What are your earliest memories of school?

Thank you.

Part 2 (4 minutes)

Interlocutor: In this part of the test, I'm going to give each of you the chance to talk for about a minute, and to comment briefly after your partner has spoken.

First, you will each have the same set of pictures to look at. They show people making music.

Indicate the pictures on page C1 to the candidates.

(Candidate A), it's your turn first. I'd like you to compare and contrast two or three of these situations, saying how the people might be feeling, and what part music might play in their lives.

Don't forget, you have about one minute for this.

All right? So, *(Candidate A)*, would you start now, please?

Candidate A: [*Approximately one minute.*]

Interlocutor: Thank you.

Now, *(Candidate B)*, can you tell us which of these people you think seems to be enjoying their music the most?

Candidate B: [*Approximately twenty seconds.*]

Interlocutor: Thank you.

Interlocutor: Now, I'm going to give each of you another set of pictures to look at. They show moments of peace and quiet.

Indicate the pictures on page C4 to the candidates.

Now, *(Candidate B)*, it's your turn. I'd like you to compare and contrast two or three of these pictures, saying how the people might be feeling, and why moments like these might be necessary in their lives.

Don't forget, you have about one minute for this.

All right? So, *(Candidate B)*, would you start now, please?

Candidate B: [*Approximately one minute.*]

Interlocutor: Thank you.

Now, *(Candidate A)*, can you tell us which picture you think best illustrates the idea of peace and quiet?

Candidate A: [*Approximately twenty seconds.*]

Interlocutor: Thank you.

Part 3 (approximately 4 minutes)

Interlocutor: Now, I'd like you to discuss something between/among yourselves, but please speak so that we can hear you.

Here are some pictures of people who have different hopes and dreams.

Indicate the pictures on pages C2 and C3 to the candidates.

Talk to each other about these people's hopes and dreams, saying how difficult it might be to make them come true, and then decide which two are most likely to become reality.

You have about four minutes for this. (Six minutes for groups of three.)

Candidates: [*Approximately four minutes. (Six minutes for groups of three.)*]

Interlocutor: Thank you.

So, which two dreams have you chosen?

Part 4 (approximately 4 minutes)

Interlocutor: *Select any of the following questions as appropriate:*

- How important is it for people to have hopes and dreams?
- What hopes for the future of the world would you like to see become reality?
- What aspects of life today would have seemed impossible to people in the past?
- Our hopes and dreams change as we get older. What differences are there between children's and adults' dreams?
- Instead of accepting the world as it is, what could we do to make it a better place?

Thank you. That is the end of the test.

Test 2

Note: In the live test, there will be both an assessor and an interlocutor in the room.

The visual material for **Test 2** appears on pages C5, C8 and C10 (Part 2), and C6 (Part 3).

Part 1   (3 minutes / 5 minutes for groups of three)

Interlocutor: Good morning (afternoon/evening). My name is ...... and this is my colleague, ...

And your names are ...... ?

Can I have your mark sheets, please?

Thank you.

First of all, we'd like to know a little about you.

(Select one or two questions and ask candidates in turn, as appropriate.)

- Where do you both/all live?
- How long have you been studying English?
- Have you been studying English together?
- What countries have you visited?

Now I'd like you to ask **each other** something about

(Select one or two prompts in any order, as appropriate.)

- things you particularly like about living in this country.
- entertainment and leisure facilities in this area.
- your reasons for studying English.
- a change you would like to make to your life in the future.

(Ask candidates one or more further questions in any order, as appropriate.)

- How important do you think English is in this country?
- How would you feel about going to live abroad permanently?
- What interesting events have happened in your life recently?
- Who do you think has had the greatest influence on your life so far? (Why?)
- What are your earliest memories of school?

Thank you.

Part 2   (6 minutes/4 minutes for pairs of candidates)

- These tasks are suitable for groups of three.
- Give one set of pictures to each candidate *in turn* and, after the final long turn, elicit comments as indicated.

Interlocutor: In this part of the test, I'm going to give each of you the chance to talk for about a minute, and to comment briefly after you both/all have spoken.

You will each have two different pictures. They show people aiming for perfection in what they are doing.

(Candidate A), it's your turn first. Here are your pictures. Please let *(Candidate(s) B (and C))* see them.

Indicate the pictures on page C5 to (Candidate A).

I'd like you to compare and contrast these pictures, saying how difficult it might have been for these people to acquire their skills, and what might have motivated them to aim for perfection.

Don't forget, you have about one minute for this.

Would you start now, please?

Candidate A: [*Approximately one minute.*]

Interlocutor: Thank you. Now, *(Candidate B)*, here are your pictures. Please let *(Candidate(s) A (and C))* see them.

Indicate the pictures on page C8 to (Candidate B).

Remember to say how difficult it might have been for these people to acquire their skills, and what might have motivated them to aim for perfection.

Would you start now, please?

Candidate B: [*Approximately one minute.*]

Interlocutor: Thank you. Now, *(Candidate C)*, here are your pictures. Again, please let *(Candidates A and B)* see them.

Indicate the pictures on page C10 to (Candidate C).

Remember to say how difficult it might have been for these people to acquire their skills, and what might have motivated them to aim for perfection.

Would you start now, please?

Candidate C: [*Approximately one minute.*]

Interlocutor: Thank you. Now, would you like to look at each other's pictures again, and say which of these people you think has put the most effort into acquiring their skills?

You have only a short time for this, so don't worry if I interrupt you.

Candidates: [*Approximately two minutes for groups of three; one minute for pairs of candidates.*]

Interlocutor: Thank you.

Part 3   (4 minutes / 6 minutes for groups of three)

Interlocutor: Now, I'd like you to discuss something between/among yourselves, but please speak so that we can hear you.

I'd like you to imagine that a leaflet is being produced to encourage people living in the cities to take more exercise. Here are some pictures which are being considered for the leaflet.

Indicate the pictures on page C6 to the candidates.

Talk to each other about how successful these pictures would be in encouraging city people to take more exercise, and then choose two pictures to include in the leaflet.

You have about four minutes for this. (Six minutes for groups of three.)

Candidates: [*Approximately four minutes. (Six minutes for groups of three.)*]

Interlocutor: Thank you.

So, which two pictures have you chosen?

Part 4   (4 minutes / 6 minutes for groups of three)

Interlocutor: *Select any of the following questions as appropriate:*

- What other ways are there of keeping fit and healthy?
- How far do you agree that you have to spend a lot of money to stay fit and healthy?
- Some people say that nowadays we are more interested in looking after ourselves than looking after others. What's your opinion?
- With new technology, people will be able to do almost anything they want to do without leaving their homes. What would the disadvantages of this be?
- Modern medicine is making it possible for people to live longer. Do you think this is a good thing? (Why (not)?)

Thank you. That is the end of the test.

Test 3

Note: In the live test, there will be both an assessor and an interlocutor in the room.

The visual material for **Test 3** appears on pages C7 and C9 (Part 2), and C11 (Part 3).

Part 1   (3 minutes)

Interlocutor: Good morning (afternoon/evening). My name is ...... and this is my colleague, ...

And your names are ...... ?

Can I have your mark sheets, please?

Thank you.

First of all, we'd like to know a little about you.

(Select one or two questions and ask candidates in turn, as appropriate.)

- Where do you both/all live?
- How long have you been studying English?
- Have you been studying English together?
- What countries have you visited?

Now I'd like you to ask **each other** something about

(Select one or two prompts in any order, as appropriate.)

- things you particularly like about living in this country.
- entertainment and leisure facilities in this area.
- your reasons for studying English.
- a change you would like to make to your life in the future.

(Ask candidates one or more further questions in any order, as appropriate.)

- How important do you think English is in this country?
- How would you feel about going to live abroad permanently?
- What interesting events have happened in your life recently?
- Who do you think has had the greatest influence on your life so far? (Why?)
- What are your earliest memories of school?

Thank you.

Part 2   (4 minutes)

Interlocutor:	In this part of the test, I'm going to give each of you the chance to talk for about a minute, and to comment briefly after your partner has spoken.
	First, you will each have the same set of pictures to look at. They show people measuring things.
	Indicate the pictures on page C7 to the candidates.
	(Candidate A), it's your turn first. I'd like you to compare and contrast two or three of these situations, saying why the people might be measuring these things, and how important it is for them to be accurate.
	Don't forget, you have about one minute for this.
	All right? So, *(Candidate A)*, would you start now, please?
Candidate A:	[*Approximately one minute.*]
Interlocutor:	Thank you.
	Now, *(Candidate B)*, can you tell us in which situation you think it is most important to be accurate?
Candidate B:	[*Approximately twenty seconds.*]
Interlocutor:	Thank you.
Interlocutor:	Now, I'm going to give each of you another set of pictures to look at. They show people exploring different environments.
	Indicate the pictures on page C9 to the candidates.
	Now, *(Candidate B)*, it's your turn. I'd like you to compare and contrast two or three of these pictures, saying what you think makes people want to explore, and what risks they may be taking.
	Don't forget, you have about one minute for this.
	All right? So, *(Candidate B)*, would you start now, please?
Candidate B:	[*Approximately one minute.*]
Interlocutor:	Thank you.
	Now, *(Candidate A)*, can you tell us which of these people you think is taking the greatest risk?
Candidate A:	[*Approximately twenty seconds.*]
Interlocutor:	Thank you.

Part 3   (approximately 4 minutes)

Interlocutor: Now, I'd like you to discuss something between/among yourselves, but please speak so that we can hear you.

Here are some pictures showing worldwide issues which worry people nowadays.

Indicate the pictures on page C11 to the candidates.

Talk to each other about these issues, saying why people find them worrying, and then decide in which two cases improvements need to be made most.

You have about four minutes for this. (Six minutes for groups of three.)

Candidates: [*Approximately four minutes. (Six minutes for groups of three.)*]

Interlocutor: Thank you.

So, which two issues have you chosen?

Part 4   (approximately 4 minutes)

Interlocutor: *Select any of the following questions as appropriate:*

- What do you think we as individuals can do to make improvements to our world?
- How important is it for us to understand different cultures and customs? (Why (not)?)
- It is a fact that today most of the world's wealth is in the hands of relatively few people. What could be done about this?
- Do you think human beings ever learn from the mistakes they have made in the past? (Why (not)?)
- One day all the nations of the world might live together peacefully. How likely do you think this is?

Thank you. That is the end of the test.

Test 4

Note: In the live test, there will be both an assessor and an interlocutor in the room.

The visual material for **Test 4** appears on pages C12, C14, C13 and C16 (Part 2), and C15 (Part 3).

Part 1   (3 minutes)

Interlocutor: Good morning (afternoon/evening). My name is ...... and this is my colleague, ...

And your names are ...... ?

Can I have your mark sheets, please?

Thank you.

First of all, we'd like to know a little about you.

(Select one or two questions and ask candidates in turn, as appropriate.)

- Where do you both/all live?
- How long have you been studying English?
- Have you been studying English together?
- What countries have you visited?

Now I'd like you to ask **each other** something about

(Select one or two prompts in any order, as appropriate.)

- things you particularly like about living in this country.
- entertainment and leisure facilities in this area.
- your reasons for studying English.
- a change you would like to make to your life in the future.

(Ask candidates one or more further questions in any order, as appropriate.)

- How important do you think English is in this country?
- How would you feel about going to live abroad permanently?
- What interesting events have happened in your life recently?
- Who do you think has had the greatest influence on your life so far? (Why?)
- What are your earliest memories of school?

Thank you.

Part 2   (4 minutes)

Interlocutor: In this part of the test, I'm going to give each of you the chance to talk for about a minute, and to comment briefly after your partner has spoken.

First, you will each have the same set of pictures to look at, but your pictures are in a different order. They show different ways of giving a presentation to an audience. Please do not show your pictures to each other.

Indicate the pictures on page C12 to Candidate A and page C14 to Candidate B.

(Candidate A), it's your turn first. I'd like you to describe **two** of these pictures, saying how the presentation is being given, and what effect the method of presentation might be having on the audience.

Don't forget, you have about one minute for this.

I'd like you, *(Candidate B)*, to listen carefully and tell us which **two** pictures have **not** been described.

All right? So, *(Candidate A)*, would you start now, please?

Candidate A:	[*Approximately one minute.*]
Interlocutor:	Thank you.

Now, *(Candidate B)*, can you tell us which two pictures *(Candidate A)* has not described?

Candidate B:	[*Approximately twenty seconds.*]
Interlocutor:	Thank you.
Interlocutor:	Now, I'm going to give each of you another set of pictures to look at. Again, they are the same pictures but in a different order. They show people working in the food business. Please do not show your pictures to each other.

Indicate the pictures on page C13 to Candidate B, and page C16 to Candidate A.

Now, *(Candidate B)*, it's your turn. I'd like you to describe **two** of these pictures, saying what the people might find satisfying about their work, and what problems they might experience.

Don't forget, you have about one minute for this.

I'd like you, *(Candidate A)*, to listen carefully and tell us which **two** pictures have **not** been described.

All right? So, *(Candidate B)*, would you start now, please?

Candidate B:	[*Approximately one minute.*]
Interlocutor:	Thank you.

Now, *(Candidate A)*, can you tell us which two pictures *(Candidate B)* has not described?

Candidate A:	[*Approximately twenty seconds.*]
Interlocutor:	Thank you.

Part 3   (approximately 4 minutes)

Interlocutor: Now, I'd like you to discuss something between/among yourselves, but please speak so that we can hear you.

Here are some pictures showing people who work in the media.

Indicate the pictures on page C15 to the candidates.

Talk to each other about what skills people might need to do these different jobs in the media, and then decide which job would be the most, and which the least, challenging.

You have about four minutes for this. (Six minutes for groups of three.)

Candidates: [*Approximately four minutes. (Six minutes for groups of three.)*]

Interlocutor: Thank you.

So, which two jobs have you chosen?

Part 4   (approximately 4 minutes)

Interlocutor: *Select any of the following questions as appropriate:*

- What attracts people to working in the media?
- Some media personalities become very famous. What problems can this bring?
- What are the advantages and disadvantages of having a large number of television channels to choose from?
- News now appears on television 24 hours a day. Do you think this is a good thing? (Why (not)?)
- Some people say satellite television has led to a loss of national identity. What's your view?

Thank you. That is the end of the test.

Marks and results

Paper 1 Reading

Candidates record their answers in pencil on a separate answer sheet. One mark is given for each correct answer to the multiple-matching tasks. Two marks are given for each correct answer to the multiple-choice and the gapped-text tasks. The total score is then weighted to 40 marks for the whole Reading paper. The Reading paper is directly scanned by computer.

Paper 2 Writing

An impression mark is awarded to each piece of writing. Examiners use band descriptions similar to the ones below to assess language and task achievement.

The **general impression mark scheme** is used in conjunction with a **task-specific mark scheme**, which focuses on criteria specific to each particular task, including relevance, length, omissions, range of structure and vocabulary, and layout; following the conventions of writing letters, reports, etc., is part of task achievement.

Allowances are made for appropriate colloquialisms and American usage and spelling.

General impression mark scheme

Band 5	Minimal errors: resourceful, controlled and natural use of language, showing good range of vocabulary and structure. Task fully completed, with good use of cohesive devices, consistently appropriate register. No relevant omissions. **NB** Not necessarily a flawless performance. Very positive effect on target reader.
Band 4	Sufficiently natural, errors only when more complex language attempted. Some evidence of range of vocabulary and structure. Good realisation of task, only minor omissions. Attention paid to organisation and cohesion; register usually appropriate. Positive effect on target reader achieved.
Band 3	*Either* (a) task reasonably achieved, accuracy of language satisfactory and adequate range of vocabulary and range of structures *or* (b) an ambitious attempt at the task, causing a number of non-impeding errors, but a good range of vocabulary and structure demonstrated. There may be minor omissions, but content clearly organised. Would achieve the required effect on target reader.
Band 2	Some attempt at task but lack of expansion and/or notable omissions or irrelevancies. Noticeable lifting of language from the input, often inappropriately. Errors sometimes obscure communication and/or language is too elementary for this level. Content not clearly organised. Would have a negative effect on target reader.
Band 1	Serious lack of control and/or frequent basic errors. Narrow range of language. Inadequate attempt at task. Very negative effect on target reader.
Band 0	(a) Fewer than 50 words per question. *or* (b) Totally illegible work. *or* (c) Total irrelevance (often a previously prepared answer to a different question).

All these comments should be interpreted at CAE level and referred to in conjunction with a task-specific mark scheme.

Paper 2 sample answers and examiner's comments

The following pieces of writing have been selected from candidates' answers. The samples relate to tasks in Tests 1–4. Explanatory notes have been added to show how the bands have been arrived at. The comments should be read in conjunction with the task-specific mark schemes included in the keys.

Sample A (Test 1, Question 1 – Letter)

Dear editor,

We are a group of students at Fordham college and would like to express our opinion to the recently published article "Council Sees Sense".

Firstly we would like to state that we are fully aware of Fordham's parking problems. Most of the students drive to college in the morning and are therefore regularly faced with the difficulties to find a parking space. The council definitely has to find a solution for this problem but we are afraid we can not agree that the transformation of Greendale Park is the best one. All of the students and the professors are regular users of the park, it is used for eating lunch there, going for short walks during the breaks and even for lessons outside in the summer. We would dare to say that Greendale Park is part of our campus life.

Apart from that the park is also of great benefit for the Fordham Residents. To prove this statement our class recently undertook a survey and conducted interviews among the residents.

The result of the survey, in which the residents were asked how often they use the park, shows clearly, that Greendale Park is frequently used. 78 percent of the Residents visit it regularly, one third of them even every day. And the interviews showed that the park is used for a variety of activities by Residents of all ages. For working people in offices Greendale Park offers a relaxing atmosphere with fresh air in an urban environment. Children have a nice place for playing outside and are safe from traffic dangers. Further many active Residents use the park for playing tennis without spending a fortune in a private club.

These arguments show that Greendale Park is the centre of the social life in Fordham and should not be turned into a car park. An alternative solution would be the building of an underground car park next to Greendale Park. Our students of Architecture and Construction Engineering have agreed to find suitable solutions for this project in their course.

We hope to hear from you.

Yours sincerely

Class A at Fordham College

Comments

Content (points covered)
Good realisation of task. All content points covered.

Organisation and cohesion
Clearly organised with attention paid to cohesion.

Range
Ambitious attempt at complex structures.

Register
Generally appropriate but slightly informal at times e.g. *we hope to hear from you*. Some awkwardness (e.g. *Dear editor*).

Accuracy
Errors sometimes occur where complex language is attempted (e.g. *difficulties to find*).

Target reader
Would be fully informed. Positive effect.

Band 4

Sample B (Test 1, Question 3 – Competition entry)

TO: INTERNATIONAL MAGAZINE.

COMPETITION TASK. *"Three things for the future."*

from: JULIA

The very first item I'd include in the capsule is a pack with lots of seeds, all kind of plants that I could possibly gather. The reason why I'd send those for the future is because the humanity is just about to lose the nature, destroing forests, hunting animals and fish, killing them, ruinning rivers and polluting the air and destroing the ozone camade. So, the idea is to give them – the men of the future – the opportunity to replant trees and plants, minimizing the effects of the mess we have been doing in this generation (the present).

The second thing is a tape, which contents shows all the wars we had in the past and all the conflicts we still have and the attomic bomb that made Yroshima desapear from the earth. Also the racism against any religion or color or diferences between nations. Perhaps they could learn with our mistakes and promote the peace and the justice and equality for every single man, giving children the right of been born and to grow up with dignity. Later to give the old man the well deserved rest and the fair place in the society.

Finally a picture of every race, at least to gather in a picture one face from every continent of this planet. Hopefully it would show them how equal we are and rise a felling of love and care among people and aproach human been from each other. Help them see how good the future can be and that depends on them. Happyness and peace are built by those hands that aim to promote, keep and reassure others lives. That is not easy, but on the other hand it's possible and it worth it.

Even if I don't win this competition I'm happy because I could express myself and whoever read my letter will have a chance to think about it all.

Comments

Content (points covered)
All points addressed.

Organisation and cohesion
Clearly paragraphed, but lacks clear introduction.

Range
Some attempt at range but marred by error.

Register
Appropriate.

Accuracy
Some impeding errors (e.g. *destroing the ozone camade, aproach human been from each other*).

Target reader
Would be slightly confused.

Band 2

Sample C (Test 2, Question 1 – Article)

O, Canada!

Do you think your English needs improvement? Do you enjoy beautiful environment, good food and friendly people? Then learning English in Canada seems to be the right solution for you! I went there for four weeks and I regret nothing. It must be said that I was quite nervous about going to a, for me, completely unknown country, all by my self, having to speak English 24 hours a day. But it turned out that my worries were totally unjustified.

To begin with, my host family were the most friendly people imaginable. I did have to share a room with the daughter but that merely made us become even closer friends. The house was lovely and they cooked absolutely delicious food! Unfortunately they didn't have much time to take me sightseeing around the city and, to be honest, the nightlife wasn't the most exciting.

What was exciting, though, was the adventurous camping trip to Rocky Mountains, were we had to cook our food over an open fire and got to see wild bears in their natural habitat.

You have to pay for your own travel costs and bring some pocket money and I must say that it was more expensive than I expected but it's definitely worth every penny! Not only do you improve your English but you make friends for life as well. When you book you also agree to host the Canadian student in your family the next year and I'm already looking forward to seeing her again!

This is something I highly recommend you to do, you can choose to go for 4–8 weeks but I would say that four weeks gives you the best value for money. Now go and book straight away and enjoy your trip to beautiful Canada!

Comments

Content (points covered)
Task fully completed, with points expanded as appropriate.

Organisation and cohesion
Very effectively organised, good use of cohesive devices.

Accuracy
Not a flawless performance, but resourceful, controlled and natural use of language.

Range
Wide range of language. Evidence of control of complex structures.

Register
Consistently appropriate. Very positive and enthusiastic.

Target reader
Would be enthused and would consider taking part.

Band 5

Sample D (Test 2, Question 4 – Text for the leaflet)

Do more sport!

It is common knowledge that sport is healthy and that everybody needs a break from time to time! Why not taking up a new sport or participating in one of the recreational activities our college provides?

The gym for example is open for everybody. For those who never trained I recommend a lesson with a sports teacher, which is for free. But there are so many other possibilities. If you like swimming you can either go to the pool on your own, with some friends, or take part in the swim-training to make it more professional. There are also some squash courts inside and some tennis courts outside. A possibility for everyone who likes running after a ball. You can book tennis-lessons at the sport secretary. For everyone who would like to take up a martial art to train his reflexes and his general condition there are three possibilities: Judo, Karate and Kung-Fu. Trainings are three times a week for every martial art. You can get further information about the timetables at the sport secretary. Everybody who likes football, basketball or hockey can sign in for the training on the Internet.

This October starts a new set of winter-sports which our college provides together with the ice-skating and curling centre 'ISCC' about five minutes on foot from here. You can participate in the ice-skating program or take up a sport the most of you have never heard of: curling.

For all the skiers and snowboarders of you: there is some further information about snowboard and ski weekends on the internet.

Good luck with your new sport!

Comments

Content (points covered)
All points covered.

Organisation and cohesion
Satisfactory organisation.

Accuracy
Some non-impeding errors (e.g. *why not taking*).

Range
Adequate.

Register
Consistently appropriate.

Target reader
Would be informed.

Band 3

Sample E (Test 3, Question 1 – Proposal)

WHAT THE FEATURE FILM SHOULD INCLUDE

INTRODUCTION

A current student of Evendine College was requested by the college principal to write this proposal to a television company on what the feature film of the college should include.

PLACES TO FILM

Filming the classrooms would be a great idea. They show tipical conversational classes, as the chairs and desks are arranged in a circle shape. This refers to the fact that everybody is envoved a part of the group.

The library seems to be the other very good choice to record. It has been modernised recently, fantastic state-of-the-art equipment helps the students besides the wide range of books.

PLACES NOT TO FILM

Unfortunately the collage does not have a sports field, not even a garden is possible, as the college is based in Central London.

It appears that the canteen is too noisy and overcrowded, so the film should not show it.

The language laboratory is being built at the moment, so there is not too much to film in this area. It should be mentioned in the interviews, though.

INTERVIEWS

For the interview one student and one teacher might be preferable. Maria is a student who could promote the college most because she has been on lots of college trips (the company might want to ask her about these), and she is a very talkative and confident girl.

Mr Brown is the favourite teacher of most students in the college. He's been teaching here for a long time, he's very intelligent and has a good sense of humour.

CONCLUSION

In short, the classrooms and the library could give an ideal picture of the college and so could the mentioned student (Maria) and teacher (Mr Brown).

Hopefully this proposal gives a better insight into what the feature film should include.

Comments

Content (points covered)
All points covered.

Organisation and cohesion
Clearly organised into paragraphs with suitable headings. Attention paid to cohesion.

Accuracy
Some non-impeding errors (e.g. *envoved, circle shape, collage*).

Range
Good range of vocabulary and structure, but awkward in places.

Register
Consistent.

Target reader
Would be informed.

Band 3

Sample F (Test 3, Question 5 – Text for the leaflet)

ASPECTS OF HEALTH AND SAFETY IN THE ILAVA HOSPITAL

Firstly, I should remind you that we work with the 'material' which is alive, with human beings. We have to make every effort to help their physical and mental necessities and keep them safe away from contageous illnesses. Furthermore, we have to keep ourselves health and safe as well.

EQUIPMENT WE USE, NEEDLES

As you surely know, except giving medicine to patient per oral, we apply injections as well. The most common accidents among nurses are uncareful and unreasonable using dirty needles. It might happen to every nurse or doctor that in the moment of putting the lid on the already used needle, she or he might accidently pinch or hurt their finger. Stay calm and do not hasitate.

HOW TO USE NEEDLES SAFELY

At first, do not forget to wear gloves. It is the most important thing which you have to keep in your mind all the time.

Secondly, after applying an injection, put immediately the lid on very carefully. Remember, there is no rush. Do not hurry to do other work you have been asked. Your health and safety is as important as health and safety of our patients. Be aware of illnesses you might meet at our ward.

WHERE TO GO AND WHAT TO DO IF THERE IS AN EMERGENCY

In case of having an accident with the already used needle, do not hesitate, wash your hands precisely and find a nurse who is in charge. Carefully follow her instruction and fill in the accident questionnare which you will be given.

Comments

Content (points covered)
All points addressed.

Organisation and cohesion
Clearly organised into headed sections.

Accuracy
A number of non-impeding errors.

Range
Some evidence of a range of language appropriate to the task.

Register
Satisfactory.

Target reader
Would be informed.

Band 3

Sample G (Test 4, Question 1 – Letter)

Dear Mr Smith,

First of all I would like to thank you for your invitation to the great opening of the Longridge Art Centre which I had the chance to attend with pleasure last night.

I must admit that I was impressed both by the event itself and the brand new premises. I am absolutely positive that immense theatre and cinema will help to promote culture among our local residents. Having spent a marvellous time in the Cafe, I still remember its unforgettable ambiance and delicious food I had the chance to try. The Art gallery surprised me with magnificent exhibition which I am going to recommend to all our students. The Arts Library, which offers wide range of art materials, is going to be one of the best sources of art knowledge for our college.

However, I noticed the lack of the recording studio which was wanted by 60% of the students. As our college contributed significantly to the building of the new Arts Centre, our students were supposed to be entitled to free use of both music and rehearsal rooms and the handout I received yesterday did not mentioned this privilege. As you probably know our college organises cinema courses focusing mainly on unusual, international films whereas the programme of your cinema includes only the latest, commercial movies which do not fit into our courses. Since the Art Centre is the only one in our region we would like to take advantage of the theatre for our annual productions and of the Arts Library. According to previous arrangements all our students had the right to 10% discount on all tickets and as far as I know nothing has changed whereas on your handout given me yesterday our students are granted only 5% discount

I am absolutely aware of the fact that the Arts Centre is a new venture and there are probably many problems to solve but I hope that the inevitable amendments will be made to improve the cooperation with our college.

We hope for further partnership relations.

Yours sincerely

The secretary of Student Committee

Comments

Content (points covered)
Candidate has omitted to suggest meeting.

Organisation and cohesion
Clear paragraphs. Good use of cohesive devices. Effective balance of positive and negative points.

Accuracy
Very few errors (e.g. *did not mentioned*, *best sources of our knowledge*).

Range
Evidence of range but with some awkwardness (e.g. *partnership relations, absolutely aware*).

Register
Wholly appropriate and consistent.

Target reader
Would not be fully informed.

Band 2

Sample H (Test 4, Question 2 – Article)

> *Our life is dominated by the mobile phones. They're everywhere. 'Ring, ring' has become a part of us. You can't hide yourself, because they will get you. People tend more to leave their wallet at home than this little toy, which is a miracle of modern technology.*
>
> *As most of our electronic equipments, the mobile phone has changed its design and its influence on our society very quickly. I remembered the time, when just the minority of the people had had one and the reason, why they had need it, was completely different. They spent a respectable amount of money and the service was limited. We made a distinction between personal and business use, because the first one wasn't very common.*
>
> *But nowadays, it is a basic tool like television and everyone in the Western World has access to it. We like to chat with friends, want to be everytime and everywhere, even in the bed being reachable. Honestly, it can be really practical, when you're late and tell it to your friends. Business people might phone home, while they're on a meeting in another city. As a result we can communicate in our complex world, efficiently and quickly.*
>
> *But, what is the strongest impact? Why do I see children of an age of ten years, writing messages rather than playing with friends? Are we too lazy and want only machines controlling our lifes? I do not hope so. Obviously there are many advantages, like saving time, fast connection and also being reachable, but on the whole: Personal contact is replaced by a new form of exchange. Then we express feelings, emotions and opinions through a machine, which reduces the miracle of the human being.*

Comments

Content (points covered)
All points addressed.

Organisation and cohesion
Organised into paragraphs, some attempt at linking.

Accuracy
A number of non-impeding errors (e.g. *electronic equipments, a respectable amount of money, why they had need*).

Range
Ambitious attempt.

Register
Consistent.

Target reader
Would be informed.

Band 3

Sample I (Test 4, Question 3 – Proposal)

To: The Organising Committee

Subject: A suitable venue for the sports event next year.

<u>Introduction</u>
The purpose of this proposal is to provide information about 'YOKOHAMA' that seems to be an ideal place to hold the sports event next year. There are wide range of accommodation, transport and entertainment for visitors.

<u>Accommodation</u>
'YOKOHAMA' is one of the biggest port cities in Japan. Numerous holidaymakers come and stay to enjoy the special atmosphere every year. They can choose appropriate accommodation according to their tastes or budgets from youth hostels to five-star hotels.

<u>Transport</u>
'YOKOHAMA' is a huge city and developed well, so several means of transportation are provided – such as tubes, trains, buses and rent-a-cars. Generally, the public transport system in Japan is very reliable. They always run punctually. In addition, the nearest international air port is 45 minutes away by bus. The only question is conjestion in rush hours, more specifically from 8.00am to 10.00am in the morning, but this could be sorted out by some regulations during the events.

<u>Entertainment</u>
'YOKOHAMA' is not only a modern city, but also a historical city. This means the city could attract anyone who have their own interests. The city use to be a capital city of Japan in 13th century so some temples built at that time still stand there. They are worth visiting. On the other hand, modern facilities – an exciting amusement park, a Marine Museum, a zoo and an art museum – are there. Should someone feel tired during their stay, she/he could ramble in a park on a hill looking onto the Tokyo Bay.
    Moreover, YOKOHAMA is next to Tokyo, a capital city of Japan. So, people could go there in half an hour by train and enjoy visiting touristic sites in Tokyo, shopping and arts – such as theatres in Japanese traditional style or modern, concerts and so on.

<u>Conclusion</u>
All in all, I have no hesitation in recommending 'YOKOHAMA' for the place where the next sports event will be held. There are no better places than YOKOHAMA, considering its excellent accommodation transport and entertainment.

Comments

Content (points covered)
All points covered. Good realisation of task.

Organisation and cohesion
Attention paid to organisation and cohesion with appropriate headings. Effective introduction and conclusion.

Accuracy
Sufficiently natural but with occasional minor slips (e.g. *The city use to be, anyone who have their own interests*) and problems with articles (e.g. *a capital city*). In places generally accurate even when more complex language attempted.

Range
Evidence of range of vocabulary (e.g. *according to their tastes or budgets*) and structure (e.g. *I have no hesitation in recommending, 45 minutes away by bus*).

Register
Appropriate.

Target reader
Positive effect. Target reader would be informed, and would consider the proposal.

Band 4

Paper 3 English in Use

One mark is given for each correct answer. The total mark is subsequently weighted to 40.

Paper 4 Listening

One mark is given for each correct question. The total for any version of the Listening paper is weighted to give a mark out of 40 for the paper.

For security reasons, several versions of the Listening paper are used at each administration of the examination. Before grading, the performance of the candidates in each of the versions is compared and marks adjusted to compensate for any imbalance in levels of difficulty.

Paper 5 Speaking

Candidates are assessed on their own individual performance and not in relation to each other, according to the following four analytical criteria: grammar and vocabulary, discourse management, pronunciation and interactive communication. These criteria are interpreted at CAE level. Assessment is based on performance in the whole test and not in particular parts of the test.

Both examiners assess the candidates. The assessor applies detailed analytical scales, and the interlocutor applies a global achievement scale, which is based on the analytical scales.

CAE typical minimum adequate performance

The candidate develops the interaction with contributions which are mostly coherent and extended when dealing with the CAE level tasks. Grammar is mostly accurate and vocabulary appropriate. Utterances are understood with very little strain on the listener.

Analytical scales

Grammar and vocabulary
This refers to the accurate and appropriate use of grammatical forms and vocabulary. It also includes the range of both grammatical forms and vocabulary. Performance is viewed in terms of the overall effectiveness of the language used.

Discourse management
This refers to the coherence, extent and relevance of each candidate's individual contribution. In this scale, the candidate's ability to maintain a coherent flow of language is assessed, either within a single utterance or a string of utterances. Also assessed here is how relevant the contributions are to what has gone before.

Pronunciation

This refers to the candidate's ability to produce comprehensible utterances to fulfil the task requirements. This includes stress, rhythm and intonation as well as individual sounds. Examiners put themselves in the position of the non-ESOL specialist and assess the overall impact of the pronunciation and the degree of effort required to understand the candidate.

Interactive communication

This refers to the candidate's ability to use language to achieve meaningful communication. This includes initiating and responding without undue hesitation, the ability to use interactive strategies to maintain or repair communication, and sensitivity to the norms of turn-taking.

Global achievement scale

This refers to the candidate's overall performance throughout the test.

Marks

Marks for each scale are awarded out of five: the assessor's marks are weighted singly and the interlocutor's mark is double-weighted. Marks for the Speaking test are subsequently weighted to produce a final mark out of 40.

Test 1 Key

Paper 1   Reading (1 hour 15 minutes)

Part 1

1 A   2 B   3 D   4 D   5 B   6 C   7 B   8 A   9 E
10 D   11 A   12 B   13 A   14 E   15 D   16 C

Part 2

17 F   18 A   19 G   20 B   21 D   22 C

Part 3

23 C   24 A   25 A   26 D   27 B

Part 4

28 E   29 C   30 B   31 A   32 C   33 C   34 E   35 B
36 B   37 E   38 A   39 C   40 D   41 C   42 C   43 D
44 A   45 A   46 E

Paper 2   Writing (2 hours)

Task-specific mark scheme

Part 1

Question 1

Content (points covered)
For Band 3 or above, candidate's **letter** must:
* respond to the article
* summarise the information from the survey
* present conclusions.

Organisation and cohesion
Letter format with opening/closing formulae. Early mention of reason for writing
and logical organisation of points.

Range
Language of evaluation, comparison, and suggestion.

Register
Formal or semi-formal. Tactful but firm and polite.

Target reader
Would be informed about how the college students and/or the local residents feel
about the decision.

Part 2

Question 2

Content (points covered)
For Band 3 or above, candidate's **article** must:
* state which two sports they most enjoy watching
* give reasons for their choice
* discuss whether sports in their country have been influenced by sports from abroad
* give reasons for this influence/lack of influence.

Organisation and cohesion
Clear organisation with appropriate paragraphing.

Range
Language of opinion.

Register
May mix registers as long as appropriate.

Target reader
Would be informed.

Question 3

Content (points covered)
For Band 3 or above, candidate's **entry** must:
* nominate three items
* explain why these items would be of interest in the future.

Organisation and cohesion
Clear paragraphing.

Range
Evaluative and descriptive language.
Range of models for future reference/recommendation etc.

Register
May mix registers, if appropriate to the approach taken by the candidate.

Target reader
Would consider the entry.

Question 4

Content (points covered)
For Band 3 or above, candidate's **report** must:
* outline strengths and weaknesses of education in their country
* suggest at least **one** future development.

Organisation and cohesion
Clear.
Headings an advantage.
Top and tail letter format acceptable.

Range
Language of opinion, assessment (perhaps suggestion/description).

Register
Unmarked – formal, but personal views acceptable.

Target reader
Would be informed.

Question 5

Content (points covered)
For Band 3 or above, candidate's **proposal** must:
- describe the company/type of company they would like to work in and why
- explain what they would like to do/will do in the company
- outline the benefits of the placement for the company.

Organisation and cohesion
Clearly ordered in paragraphs. Memo/letter layout acceptable.

Range
Language of business.

Register
Formal to unmarked.

Target reader
Would be informed and would consider the proposal.

Paper 3 **English in Use** (1 hour 30 minutes)

Part 1

1 C 2 A 3 D 4 B 5 C 6 A 7 C 8 D 9 C
10 A 11 C 12 B 13 D 14 D 15 C

Part 2

16 our 17 in/during 18 which/that 19 even/Even 20 be 21 instead
22 who 23 themselves 24 have 25 at 26 how 27 us 28 this
29 as 30 the

Part 3

31 varieties 32 reference 33 different,'/different', 34 bought 35
Portuguese 36 ✓ 37 successful 38 of, 39 along 40 immediately
41 lead 42 customers 43 Olvero, 44 ✓ 45 ✓ 46 future.

Part 4

47 enthusiasm 48 product 49 truly 50 evolution 51 inclusion
52 persuasive 53 increasingly 54 traditionally 55 resourceful
56 apparently 57 factual 58 primarily 59 uninterrupted 60 manufacturers
61 wrapping

Part 5

62 too complicated/too complex/too confusing/from obvious   63 follow/understand/
comprehend/get   64 he deserves/he should/he merits   65 too often/excessively/too
much/too frequently   66 believe in/believe/take seriously   67 boring/predictable/NOT
tedious   68 walk out/get out   69 wrong parts/wrong roles   70 too loud/too noisy
71 be seen   72 new ideas   73 professional   74 keen on/enthusiastic about/fond of/
crazy about/devoted to/happy with

Part 6

75 E   76 A   77 H   78 D   79 B   80 F

Paper 4   Listening (approximately 45 minutes)

Part 1

1 international (golf) competition(s)/golf internationally   2 (the) landowners/ land (-)
owners   3 championship   4 (the) cities/(the) towns/(the) urban areas/ the city
5 (urban) parks/a park   6 grow fast/quickly   7 (a) nature reserve(s)/a place for
children to see animals and trees   8 (local) community/(local) communities

Part 2

9 familiar (faces and other)   10 (written) diaries/diary   11 (up) lots of/a lot of
film(s)/many films/plenty of film(s)/many rolls of film(s)   12 throw away/out the/get rid
of/dispose of (the)   13 positions/places/angles   14 sky   15 (camera) setting(s)
16 level/height

Part 3

17 D   18 B   19 A   20 C   21 D   22 B
23 C   24 D

Part 4

25 D   26 G   27 F   28 H   29 B   30 F   31 H   32 G   33 D
34 B

Transcript   *This is the Cambridge Certificate in Advanced English, Listening Test. Test
One.*

*This paper requires you to listen to a selection of recorded material and
answer the accompanying questions.*

*There are four parts to the test. You will hear Part Two **once** only. All the
other parts of the test will be heard twice.*

*There will be a pause before each part to allow you to look through the
questions, and other pauses to let you think about your answers. At the end
of every pause you will hear this sound.*

tone

*You should write your answers in the spaces provided on the **question** paper. You will have **ten minutes** at the end to **transfer your answers to the separate answer sheet.***

There will now be a pause. You must ask any questions now, as you will not be allowed to speak during the test.

[pause]

PART 1

Now open your question paper and look at Part One.

[pause]

You will hear part of a lecture in which a man called Tom Trueman talks about golf courses and the environment. For questions 1 to 8 complete the sentences.

You will hear the recording twice. You now have 30 seconds in which to look at Part One.

[pause]

tone

Lecturer: Good afternoon. I'm here to talk about the rather delicate question of golf courses in the countryside. I want to look at the growth of golf in this country and make some suggestions regarding its future development.

A few years ago, a report was published by the body that governs the sport nationally. At that time, the popularity of golf was expanding rapidly on the back of all the publicity surrounding the success of certain local golfers in international competitions.

The report said that people who didn't belong to existing golf clubs, but who wanted to start playing the game, found that there simply weren't enough facilities to go round. So, the report concluded, around 700 courses would have to be built to meet the demand.

Following that report, there was, as you can imagine, enormous interest amongst landowners, not to mention businessmen, who suddenly realised that there was money to be made out of golf. Now, the ordinary beginner couldn't really afford to pay for a high standard of facilities, but, for some reason, developers tended to build championship golf courses, so that quite a few of the hundreds built across the country failed financially.

And, of course, not everybody likes golf courses anyway. They cause changes to the local environment and are used only by those with money, and that often means people driving out from the cities, rather than the local population.

A further objection to golf courses is that, although they don't involve much building, the smooth close-cut grass gives them the ordered appearance of urban parks, because developers seem to be obsessed with the idea of stripping everything out and starting again. The land is levelled out, then artificial bumps are introduced, alien species of plants, often imported from abroad, are put in; trees that grow fast are particularly popular, as are new varieties of grass that provide a good walking surface. And, of course, this means that wild animals and other forms of native wildlife are uprooted and suffer as a result.

But my point is why should all this destruction be necessary? Why do all golf courses have to look the same? I believe that, with a little bit of imagination, many courses could easily be turned into nature reserves, where interesting or rare plant varieties could be preserved. Many of the arguments raised by the critics would be answered in this way and I think this is an approach that should be considered before any more golf courses are built in this country. Most importantly, courses should be designed to attract rather than drive away wildlife. A knock-on effect of this would be another layer of use, as schoolchildren and others could come to study the natural habitats that would be preserved, making the golf course much more an integral part of the local community as well as the local ecology.

So, what can ...

[pause]

tone

Now you will hear the recording again.

[The recording is repeated.]

[pause]

That is the end of Part One.

[pause]

PART 2   *Part Two*

You will hear a radio talk given by a photographer. For questions 9 to 16, complete the sentences.

*Listen very carefully as you will hear the recording **once** only. You now have 45 seconds in which to look at Part Two.*

[pause]

tone

Interviewer: It's a task that usually takes only a fraction of a second, yet the results of taking just one photograph can be magical. Ian Hasson is lucky enough to earn a living taking pictures, but for many of us, it's just a hobby that we'd like to be better at. Here's Ian with a few useful tips.

Ian: If you're like most of the amateur photographers that I come across, then it isn't pictures of famous celebrities that you're interested in, but rather pictures of familiar faces or places that induce groans of 'oh no' when you show them off. And you want to put these familiar scenes in an album with a little penned note beneath each one ... because these days, photography has taken over from written diaries and the idea of capturing moments in time has become pictorial ... our photo albums have become a kind of diary for us.

Unfortunately, it isn't as simple as 'take a shot – put it in the album'. What many people don't realise is that whatever your focus is – people or scenery or whatever – you've got to be prepared to use up lots of film. You won't get a great shot the first time. When you get all your films back from being developed – then it's important to throw away the ones that aren't any good ...

if you put everything in an album, the bad ones really do detract from the better ones. You've got to get rid of them. Then you can show off the prize shots.

How do you get these? Well the advice itself can be pretty straightforward. If you're trying to do landscapes, for example, then I think you should try a variety of positions. Get down on your knees or ... stand on a rock or something. Also you can try varying your main focus ... take the view with plenty of sky and then do the opposite – try it with hardly any sky. Shoot lots and make sure that the pictures are as sharp as you can get them.

As for shots of people or portrait photos, have a good look at all the camera settings before you even mention to your friends that you're about to take a photo. For example, if you need it, is the flash on? If you spend a lot of time messing around with the settings, you'll end up with a picture of someone looking fed up.

With children, you've really got to avoid getting them to pose at all, in fact you'll get the best shots if they're completely unaware. Also, to avoid distortion, you've got to get down to their level. Sit or kneel so that you're the same height as they are. And remember, it doesn't matter whether everything else is in focus as long as the subject's eyes are sharp. So start focusing on the eyes and everything else should be OK.

[pause]

That is the end of Part Two.

[pause]

PART 3

Part Three

You will hear an interview on a train with two friends, Jane and Chris, chefs who both won prizes in the National Railway Chef of the Year competition. For questions 17 to 24, choose the correct answer A, B, C or D.

You will hear the recording twice. You now have one minute in which to look at Part Three.

[pause]

tone

Greg: Serving more than 200,000 meals a year would be a challenge for any chef, but step up constraints of time, space and a demand for culinary excellence and you have the life of a railway chef. Chris and Jane, the idea of having to cook in cramped surroundings, with limited ingredients and a very tight schedule, as you did in the recent competition, must have been a terrifying prospect ...

Chris: Well, hardly – I actually operate under those restrictions every day!

Jane: That's true, of course, we both do – but there's always the added danger that things can go wrong, and the challenge of preparing a top-quality, three-course meal for four – which costs no more than £50 – and in front of all those judges!

Greg: Well, Jane, you were a runner up and Chris came first. I gather you faced some stiff competition from the other finalists.

Jane: No doubt about that. All the chefs who entered the competition were brilliant in their own way – but someone has to win! But the real problem is trying to be creative as the train hurtles through the countryside at over 100 miles an hour – there's little room for mistakes – and you have to be able to keep your balance!

Chris: Actually, I'd only been a railway chef for three months. And I can tell you that life on board is no easy ride. There's no nipping out to get the extra bunch of parsley, or a lemon.

Greg: But you're used to working under pressure all the same, aren't you? How do you set about being organised?

Chris: You've just got to make sure you're focused on the job. Being able to keep an eye on a dozen things at once is also an advantage!

Greg: But do you actually enjoy what you're doing?

Jane: There's plenty of scope to express yourself as a chef in the job – and the open kitchen means that customers will often compliment you personally on the food. That's one of the biggest highlights of the job.

Chris: I'd certainly go along with that. Very few restaurant chefs have the chance to experience that.

Greg: And what about the menus, who decides what to cook?

Jane: They're decided in advance for the whole railway network by two extremely famous chefs, who are actually brothers. I suppose we both find it restricting.

Chris: Hmm. I do get a bit frustrated from time to time – think I could be a little more adventurous – but it's all a question of adaptability – which I suspect Jane is better at than I am!

Jane: Not at all – I can be quite inflexible when the mood takes me!

Greg: So what would be a typical routine for you both?

Chris: You have to start at around 5.30 in the morning – check that all the ingredients have been delivered – then it's a mad rush to get everything ready.

Jane: And precious little time to rest any other time during the day, as you often have to set tables on other trains and help other staff. Timing's particularly tight, you see. In other restaurants orders come in and go out over two or three hours, but we have to turn round before the passengers reach their stations. It's all a bit nerve-racking.

Greg: So what motivated you to do this in the first place?

Chris: I've been on the move ever since I left college. So when I got engaged, I decided it was time to settle down. So when I saw this job, it seemed a reasonable compromise between personal commitments and my reluctance to stay in one place.

Jane: For me it was something that just caught my eye – not just ordinary run of the mill stuff. And, if you get the time, you get a good view out of the windows!

Greg: And how do you stop things from spilling over when the train moves?

Chris: It's not a problem for me. I was a chef on a liner, so I've got plenty of experience of cookery in motion!

Jane: Yes, but I think it helps if you only half fill saucepans with boiling water – even so, they often spill over and you start saying nasty things to yourself about the driver – and it's not usually his fault!

Chris: Let's just say that you quickly learn not to put things under the grill without keeping an eye on them!

Greg: Has either of you had any major disasters?

Chris: [laughs] I'd only been in the job for three days and I had this huge roast in the oven. I opened the door, turned around for a moment, distracted, I suppose, and it just flew out. Fortunately it landed in the sink, so it was okay.

Greg: And what qualities would you say it was necessary for a railway chef to have?

Jane: From my point of view, dedication and determination – you won't get anywhere without these!

Chris: And, let's admit it – a sense of humour. There have been times when I would have resigned long ago if I hadn't had that!

Greg: And what of the future?

Chris: Who knows? – perhaps the first chef on a trip to the Moon?

Jane: Now, that would be a challenge! But somehow, I doubt I'll be with you on that one. I'm terrified of flying!

Greg: Well, now, if you don't mind, we thought our listeners might be interested in the recipes for your prize-winning meals ...

[pause]

tone

Now you will hear the recording again.

[The recording is repeated.]

[pause]

That is the end of Part Three.

[pause]

PART 4

Now look at the fourth and last part of the test. Part Four consists of two tasks.

You will hear five short extracts in which different people are talking about works of art they would buy if they had £20,000. Look at Task One. For questions 25 to 29, match the extracts as you hear them with the works of art the people would buy, listed A to H. Now look at Task Two. For questions 30 to 34, match the extracts as you hear them with the comment each speaker makes about the world of art, listed A to H.

You will hear the recording twice. While you listen you must complete both tasks. You now have 40 seconds to look at Part Four.

[pause]

tone

Speaker One: If the money were handed to me on a plate, then I'd go and look at all sorts of places – for things like drawings and watercolours of a bygone age. The money would go further in the non-contemporary field. You have to pay an awful lot for oil paintings but you certainly get the best prices at sales, where they always have bright, colourful catalogues giving you all sorts of information about the paintings, although you might miss something vital if you don't read the small print! Naturally, you have to be careful – you wouldn't want to buy a forgery! You need a good eye to spot something authentic – it's not always that obvious at first sight.

Speaker Two: I can't think of anything nicer than having lots of money to spend on art. The only question is whether I'd go for the big one or spread it around! I'd probably go for a single collection of drawings I came across at an exhibition by a modern artist a short while ago. Actually, a few years ago, I acquired a painting quite cheaply by an artist who now sells for thousands but you should never buy art with the intention of turning it into a money-spinner. In my opinion, art should be accessible – not something remote and unreachable – and not something hidden away from the public eye.

Speaker Three: Collecting works of art is my passion – but, to be frank, you need space. Every single corner of my small house is jam-packed with paintings – so I'm not sure where I'd put any new ones! But, if I saw something I liked, I'd just have to have it. No matter where it goes! I'd like a landscape – particularly one from another country – but not necessarily an old master. I really regret not buying more when I was younger but at the time I just couldn't find the ready cash. I'd be a millionaire by now if I'd followed my instincts! That's what being a real collector means. Even if your furniture has to disappear!

Speaker Four: I'm what you might call a sort of professional. I'm a kind of, well, art middleman. I buy catalogues from all the best dealers. So if I had that kind of money to spend, I'd do what I always do: think what's going to sell well – buy it, then rent it out for exhibitions. The secret is to buy first works from those artists who haven't really found their style. To be honest, that's the kind of thing I like to see hanging on my own walls – but to succeed, as it were, it also helps if you have a good eye for a money-spinner – and a bit of luck!

Speaker Five: If I were given a sum of money like that, I'd buy something eye-catching, something that everyone would notice – even if they didn't like it! I'd probably go for a giant statue that I would place in my hallway, or in a park near my house. There's only one reason to collect a work of art: because you love the image and you want to live with it forever and there has to be some kind of message as well. It's not just about investing money or making a fortune. I always think it's amazing that many great artists didn't even become famous until after they died.

[pause]

tone

Now you will hear the recording again. Remember you must complete both tasks.

[The recording is repeated.]

[pause]

*That is the end of Part Four. There will now be a ten-minute pause to allow you to **transfer your answers to the separate answer sheet**. Be sure to follow the numbering of all the questions. The question papers and answer sheets will then be collected by your supervisor.*

[Teacher, pause the recording here for ten minutes. Remind your students when they have one minute left.]

That is the end of the test.

Test 2 Key

Paper 1   Reading (1 hour 15 minutes)

Part 1

1 D	2 C	3 B	4 B	5 D	6 C	7 A	8 B	9 D
10 A	11 B	12 A	13 D	14 C	15 B	16 A		

Part 2

17 D	18 B	19 G	20 E	21 A	22 C

Part 3

23 D	24 B	25 C	26 A	27 B	28 D

Part 4

29 E	30 A	31 B	32 A	33 D	34 C	35 E	36 B
37 A	38 C	39 D	40 E	41 D	42 B	43 E	44 C
45 A	46 D	47 C					

Paper 2   Writing (2 hours)

Task-specific mark scheme

Part 1

Question 1

Content (points covered)
For Band 3 or above, the candidate's **article** must:
- describe what candidate enjoyed about exchange programme
- outline any problem(s)
- encourage reader to take part.

Organisation and cohesion
Clear paragraphing. Letter format acceptable with appropriate opening and closing formulae.

Range
Language of description and persuasion.

Register
May mix registers if appropriate to approach taken by candidate.

Target reader
The editor would consider printing the article. The reader would be interested and consider enrolling on the programme.

Part 2

Question 2

Content (points covered)
For Band 3 or above, the candidate's **application** must:
- describe the type(s) of music suggested for festival
- describe the candidate's own musical tastes
- suggest why the candidate should be employed as a judge.

Organisation and cohesion
Letter layout with appropriate opening and closing formulae. Clearly paragraphed.

Range
Language of description, explanation and recommendation.
Vocabulary of music.

Register
Consistently formal or unmarked.

Target reader
Would be informed and consider the application.

Question 3

Content (points covered)
For Band 3 or above, the candidate's **contribution** must:
- mention at least two jobs
- refer to pay and/or conditions
- refer to possible problems.

Organisation and cohesion
Clearly organised into paragraphs.

Range
Language of explanation and advice.

Register
Consistently formal, unmarked or informal.

Target reader
Would be informed and would consider the contribution for the guide book.

Question 4

Content (points covered)
For Band 3 or above, the candidate's **text for the leaflet** must:
- include information about facilities and/or activities
- point out benefits of taking up opportunities
- encourage readers to use facilities/join in activities.

Organisation and cohesion
Clearly organised into paragraphs.
Headings would be an advantage.

Range
Vocabulary relevant to facilities/activities chosen.

Register
Unmarked or informal.

Target reader
Would be informed about facilities/activities on offer and their benefits and feel encouraged to participate.

Question 5

Content (points covered)
For a Band 3 or above, the candidate's **letter** must:
- give a brief introduction to the company
- describe the day/programme
- refer to the (good) working practices the group will see/learn.

Organisation and cohesion
Letter layout with appropriate opening and closing formulae.

Range
Language of description, explanation and vocabulary appropriate to the world of work.

Register
Consistently unmarked or formal.

Target reader
Would be informed.

Paper 3 English in Use (1 hour 30 minutes)

Part 1

1 A   2 D   3 C   4 D   5 A   6 B   7 B   8 D   9 D
10 B   11 C   12 B   13 D   14 C   15 A

Part 2

16 at   17 of   18 whose   19 them/others/these   20 has   21 their
22 it   23 one   24 too   25 on   26 is   27 how   28 any
29 have   30 when/if

Part 3

31 caught up   32 ✓   33 accompaniment   34 relatively   35 adaptable
36 years or   37 ✓   38 today's   39 tougher   40 struggling   41 ✓
42 desperate   43 attempted   44 heroes   45 ✓   46 disastrous

Part 4

47 scientifically   **48** sweetness   **49** desirable   **50** preference   **51** availability
52 healthier   **53** addictive   **54** relaxation   **55** reasonably   **56** spacious
57 tastefully   **58** imaginative/unimaginable   **59** chosen   **60** unforgettable
61 memorable

Part 5

62 present/the moment   **63** accept/realise   **64** evidence to/proof to/documentation to/
receipt to/document(s) to/NOT paper/certificate   **65** department/personnel/workers
66 not appear/arrive/NOT revolve/move/turn, etc.   **67** informed/notified/advised/NOT
wrote   **68** the same   **69** looked into/investigated/gone into/examined/explored/worked
on   **70** locate/recover/get back/ retrieve/return   **71** compensate/reimburse
72 content(s)   **73** approximate/estimated/possible/actual
74 contact/ring/phone/telephone

Part 6

75 D   **76** F   **77** A   **78** I   **79** C   **80** E

Paper 4   Listening (approximately 45 minutes)

Part 1

1 Her parents/family//Helen(')s parents/family   **2** remembering/memorising/learning
(her/the lines) (by heart)   **3** (throat) operation   **4** (great) comedy (actress/actor)/comic/
comedian/comedienne   **5** (a) perfume(s)/scent(s)   **6** letters/correspondence
7 (reading) (the) reviews   **8** (her/the) audience(s)

Part 2

9 (things like) (tourist) guidebooks (for tourists) ACCEPT guide books
10 Chinese (food/meals) NOT misspelling of Chinese   **11** original/different
12 sweet(s) (course)/pudding(s) (course)/dessert(s) (course)   **13** (any foreign word(s)/words
in (a) foreign language(s)/other languages/another language/foreign names ALLOW foreign
vocabulary/vocabulary in (a) foreign language(s)   **14** (good) value (for money)
15 (a) recommendation(s)   **16** different/special treatment

Part 3

17 D   **18** D   **19** A   **20** B   **21** A   **22** A

Part 4

23 E   **24** D   **25** C   **26** A   **27** H   **28** E   **29** G   **30** B   **31** D
32 C

Transcript *This is the Cambridge Certificate in Advanced English Listening Test. Test Two.*

This paper requires you to listen to a selection of recorded material and answer the accompanying questions.

*There are four parts to the test. You will hear Part Two **once** only. All the other parts of the test will be heard twice.*

There will be a pause before each part to allow you to look through the questions, and other pauses to let you think about your answers. At the end of every pause you will hear this sound.

tone

*You should write your answers in the spaces provided on the **question** paper. You will have **ten** minutes at the end to **transfer your answers to the separate answer sheet.***

There will now be a pause. You must ask any questions now, as you will not be allowed to speak during the test.

[pause]

PART 1   *Now open your question paper and look at Part One.*

[pause]

You will hear part of a radio programme in which an expert on theatre history is talking about the life of a famous actress called Helen Perry. For questions 1 to 8, complete the sentences.

You will hear the recording twice. You now have 30 seconds in which to look at Part One.

[pause]

tone

Presenter: We have in the studio today Vernon Hall, an expert on theatre history, to tell us all about Helen Perry, one of the greatest actresses of all time.

Vernon: Helen Perry was born in 1847, right in the middle of the nineteenth century, when the theatre was the main form of public entertainment. Her acting career didn't actually get off to a very promising start, which was not surprising given that acting was considered an unsuitable career for a young woman. So she waited until she was 22 before going on stage to avoid her parents' disapproval.

   Once on the stage, she found that she had other problems. Although her first part was very small, she had great trouble learning the lines and, according to her, this was something she found difficult throughout her acting career. However, this did not prevent her from becoming an incredibly successful actress. People who saw her act said that the thing that made her so special was her voice – apparently, it had an almost hypnotic quality. However, it nearly brought her career to an abrupt end when she was in her fifties. Her voice just got lower and huskier and she quite often lost it when she had a cold. Finally she had a very risky throat operation – which paid off, because she went on acting for another 25 years after that.

Helen Perry is now remembered as a great classical actress but she was actually very skilful. She was, for example, a great comedy actress which was what really gave her broad popular appeal. And she was immensely popular. At the height of her fame, people could buy all sorts of mementos like postcards and paperweights with her picture on. She was one of the first stars to have a perfume named in her honour, and that brand, simply called 'Helen', remained on sale until quite recently.

It's always been known that several famous plays were written for her, but what isn't so well-known is that she had literary talent herself because we have the letters she exchanged with one writer and they show she had great style and wit.

Some people feel that she should have retired earlier, when she was at her peak, but personally, I disagree. We have no film of her acting, of course, but from the reviews of her performances towards the end of her career we can see that although she had difficulty walking, she is still described as magnetic.

She picked up quite a few honorary degrees from various universities, something which had never happened to an actress before. She was pleased to get academic recognition, of course, but what <u>really</u> pleased her was the way that the audiences loved her, and that was all the recognition she really needed. She'll certainly never be forgotten.

[pause]

tone

Now you will hear the recording again.

[The recording is repeated]

[pause]

That is the end of Part One.

[pause]

PART 2

Part Two

You will hear a talk given by Norma Tainton, a journalist who writes reviews of restaurants. For questions 9 to 16, complete the sentences.

*Listen very carefully as you will hear the recording **once** only. You now have 45 seconds in which to look at Part Two.*

[pause]

tone

Journalist: Good evening. My name's Norma Tainton. I'm a journalist and I write a regular newspaper column which features reviews of the restaurants where I've been eating recently. I also contribute to things like guidebooks which provide reviews of restaurants for tourists. Although I did once try to write a cookery book, I've never really been involved in the restaurant trade as such, I'm primarily just a writer with an interest in food.

So what does the job involve? Well, it means eating out six days a week and people wonder how I cope and, of course, it is important to try and eat a different type of meal each day. If it's fish today, then it'll be a curry or pasta tomorrow for example, and while I'm particularly fond of Chinese food, it'd be a mistake to have a Chinese meal too often.

I'm particularly interested in dishes where the chef has done something original; there's no point just having a steak and salad because there'd be nothing to write about. Also important for me is eating with someone. That way I get to see other things from the menu, plus someone else's impression of the place. I also tend to rely on my guests to try the puddings too, because that really isn't my sort of thing, although I might just try a spoonful of a sweet to get an idea.

I always carry a notebook in my handbag, but I don't take notes during the meal, preferring to scribble down my ideas when I get home. Sometimes though, I need to note down any foreign words, because it'd be embarrassing to get things wrong in another language.

Of course, I don't have to pay for the meals I eat, but I try nonetheless to think about the price in terms of value for money. I think that's the most important service I can offer my readers. When it comes to the food, service, atmosphere and so on, I can only give my opinions. They decide if the whole package is worth spending their money on, so I don't make recommendations as such, I just offer factual information, rather than specifically recommending any one place.

One thing people always say to me is that surely I'm now so well known that I get special treatment in restaurants. But nobody knows I'm coming because I book a table under another name, so I don't receive different treatment from anyone else.

People often ask me if there's one memorable meal …

[pause]

That is the end of Part Two.

[pause]

PART 3   *Part Three*

You will hear a radio interview with the writer, Tom Davies. For questions 17 to 22, choose the correct answer A, B, C or D.

You will hear the recording twice. You now have one minute in which to look at Part Three.

[pause]

tone

Interviewer: My guest today is Tom Davies. He has written a series of highly-acclaimed novels, as well as a play and two successful filmscripts. He has said, 'I love the solitude, the sheer pleasure of writing, the secret excitement.' Tom, writing is a solitary business, but does it go on being exciting?

Tom Davies: Well, writing is an exciting process, although there are good days and bad days, obviously. I remember when I started, I used to sweat for so long over one sentence that it really wasn't much of a pleasure. But I got past that stage and yes, I do find that when things go well, when things are working out, it is very absorbing.

Interviewer: But surely less secret these days, now that you've won major prizes?

Tom Davies: Possibly. I recently read out a whole chunk of my work-in-progress at a literary festival because it's one way of trying these things out, whereas in the past I'd been too frightened that if I talked about what I was writing, I would somehow lose control of it. But I think generally I don't talk about what I am intending to write, because I'm still not entirely sure myself which way it's going to go. But once something is down in a first or second draft, then you can try it out and see how it sounds.

Interviewer: And you've said that at any one time there are as many as ten or fifteen ideas for novels floating around in your head. How do you choose which one to follow up?

Tom Davies: You've got to find the idea that's got the right kind of urgency and it's not a rational decision. It's patience and luck and turning up at your desk every morning even when nothing seems to be coming. If you're not there, then nothing is precisely what will happen. But once I get started, then a good day would be two or three hundred words.

Interviewer: And then do you hone it, do you go back over it?

Tom Davies: I go back all the time until I get to the stage when I won't look at it again because you need the distance of time to look back and see it from a different perspective.

Interviewer: And is there anyone who you can then give this manuscript to and say, 'Look, before I go any further, tell me what you think of this.'?

Tom Davies: I give the finished draft to certain old friends who're permitted to be as brutal as they like. That's very useful because I think there's a danger for writers as they get older, as their reputations get established, that publishers won't tell them if they've any serious doubts about a piece. So sceptical friends are very important to give you the benefit of a truthful opinion.

Interviewer: And you trust these friends?

Tom Davies: Absolutely. The first time I tried this, years ago, a friend of mine said, 'Look, I think this novel's absolutely terrible, put it in a drawer and forget about it.' And I didn't speak to him for eighteen months. But after that I learnt that if you give someone your novel to read, you've got to allow them to say that kind of thing. These days I wouldn't take it so personally.

Interviewer: And although you've denied any suggestion that you write about yourself, there are actually all sorts of bits and pieces of you dotted all over your work, aren't there?

Tom Davies: Someone said that you can't write two hundred words in a novel without giving something of yourself away and I suppose that's true. Perhaps that's why I've always been a bit defensive about my work.

Interviewer: Now, despite those two successful filmscripts, you haven't, strangely, had a lot of luck translating your stories onto the big screen, have you? Why's that?

Tom Davies: Oh well, my first experience was of a low-budget English film. And because we had so little money to work with, it was wonderfully uncomplicated and I thought, 'Oh what a brilliant life. I could write novels and then in between each one, I could do a film.'

Interviewer: Because it's so much easier?

Tom Davies:	Well, it was such fun being away on location surrounded by fabulously competent people, all taking fierce pride in their ability to do something so well and very quickly. The panic of the ticking clock, the things going wrong and then somehow being solved at the last minute, all that was marvellous for someone who usually spends his time locked up in an empty room.
Interviewer:	So it's actually harder to write a good screenplay?
Tom Davies:	No, I wouldn't say that. Indeed, I don't think a screenplay is a literary form in itself. It's more a set of instructions, a bit like a recipe. And you can fool yourself into thinking that you can see what's going to be on the screen, but actually too many people intervene in the finished product, you're just a part of the process, so it's quite unlike a novel where you're in sole charge, as it were.
Interviewer:	Tom, there, unfortunately, we have to leave it. Thank you …

[pause]

tone

Now you will hear the recording again.

[The recording is repeated.]

[pause]

That is the end of Part Three.

[pause]

PART 4   *Now look at the fourth and last part of the test. Part Four consists of two tasks.*

You will hear five short extracts in which different people are reading from their autobiographies. Look at Task One. For questions 23 to 27, match the extracts as you hear them with what each speaker is saying, listed A to H. Now look at Task Two. For questions 28 to 32, match the extracts with the feeling each speaker expresses, listed A to H.

You will hear the recording twice. While you listen you must complete both tasks. You now have 30 seconds in which to look at Part Four.

[pause]

tone

Speaker One:	So there I was, all of a sudden it had all happened for me. All those years of struggle, to become 'an overnight success'. 'Lucky you!' my friends said, but luck didn't come into it, just perseverance in the face of all the rejection. And did it all seem worth it now? Now that I'd finally made it? Well, I didn't have much time to get carried away with it all. The record company wanted the next record. How was I going to follow it? Had I used up all my inspiration? Was I just a 'one-hit-wonder', destined to be instantly forgotten? These thoughts kept me awake at night.
Speaker Two:	That day the phone never stopped ringing. Everyone wanted to know, 'Have you seen the paper?' Well, imagine what it's like to have your photograph plastered all over the front page with a story like that. 'TV star in police

161

enquiry' it said and the article was full of things they'd just made up, and plain lies. Well, it hadn't happened to me before and I wasn't really ready for it, but I thought, 'Well, that's the way it goes. It's the price of fame, as they say. I won't even bother denying such a load of rubbish.' So I didn't react and pretty soon the whole thing had blown over.

Speaker Three: I suppose I first realised what had happened when I went to my regular restaurant and instead of showing me to 'my table', the head waiter asked me if I'd booked. I suppose most people would have got depressed but in a funny sort of way I was glad. I thought, 'I've made my money and now there's a new generation of comedians taking over and people don't find me funny any more.' But I'm not going to miss it, all those people coming up to you in shops and expecting you to be funny all the time, all those idiots telling you jokes in restaurants. Oh, it'll be bliss not to have to put up with that any more.

Speaker Four: So then I had to tell the others. We'd known each other since we were kids, we'd formed the band in our teens and now I was going to tell them I was going solo. But I knew it was exactly the right thing for me to do at that time. We were right at the top and the only way was down. And anyway, I'd got the feeling they'd had about enough – all that touring, it was wearing us all out. So I figured they wouldn't take it badly – in a way they'd be glad I'd made the decision for them. And I was looking forward to taking up a new challenge.

Speaker Five: The next day it began to sink in. My big break, my first major role in a major film and I'd let it go. It was a strange feeling. I mean, I should have been devastated but the more I thought about it, the more I realised they'd only been taking me for a ride. Just because I was a relative unknown, they'd thought they could get me on the cheap. Well, I thought, nobody treats me like that. I was right to tell them what they could do with their lousy offer. What a cheek! I almost rang them back to give them a piece of my mind but I thought better of it. Still, better parts'll come my way soon, I said to myself, and I was right.

[pause]

tone

Now you will hear the recording again. Remember you must complete both tasks.

[The recording is repeated.]

[pause]

*That is the end of Part Four. There will now be a ten-minute pause to allow you to **transfer your answers to the separate answer sheet**. Be sure to follow the numbering of all the questions. The question papers and answer sheets will then be collected by your supervisor.*

[Teacher, pause the recording here for ten minutes. Remind your students when they have one minute left.]

That is the end of the test.

Test 3 Key

Paper 1   Reading (1 hour 15 minutes)

Part 1

1 C   2 B   3 A   4 D   5 D   6 C   7 A   8 C   9 A
10 C   11 B   12 C

Part 2

13 F   14 A   15 E   16 G   17 C   18 B

Part 3

19 A   20 B   21 C   22 D   23 C   24 D

Part 4

25 B   26 C   27 A   28 D   29 C   30 B   31 C   32 D
33 A   34 C   35 D   36 C   37 D   38 B   39 A   40 D
41 B   42 D   43 C   44 A   45 C

Paper 2   Writing (2 hours)

Task-specific mark scheme

Part 1

Question 1

Content (points covered)
For Band 3 or above, the candidate's **proposal** must:
• explain which aspects of college should be filmed
• suggest interviewees
• justify choice.
NB acceptable to address proposal to Principal.

Organisation and cohesion
Clear paragraphing or sections with suitable linking. Headings may be an advantage. Letter format acceptable with appropriate opening and closing formulae.

Range
Language of suggestion and justification.

Register
If addressed to TV company, consistently formal or unmarked.
If addressed to Principal, any as long as consistent.

Target reader
Would be informed.

Part 2

Question 2

Content (points covered)
For Band 3 or above, the candidate's **article** must:
- discuss one issue (either work, education or the environment) in depth
- relate this to young people.

Organisation and cohesion
Clearly paragraphed. Use of linking devices.

Range
Language of explanation and argument.

Register
May mix registers if appropriate to approach taken by candidate.

Target reader
Would be informed and consider publishing article.

Question 3

Content (points covered)
For Band 3 or above, the candidate's **reference** must:
- indicate how long they have known the person
- describe the person's character
- explain why the person would be suitable for the job.

Organisation and cohesion
Clear organisation with appropriate paragraphing.

Range
Language of description, explanation and reasoning. Vocabulary of character and of work.

Register
Consistently formal or unmarked.

Target reader
Would be informed and consider application.

Question 4

Content (points covered)
For Band 3 or above, the candidate's **competition entry** must:
- describe one leisure facility
- explain why it is needed
- explain which groups in the community would benefit.

Organisation and cohesion
Clear paragraphing.

Range
Language of description, opinion and explanation.

Register
May mix registers if appropriate to approach taken by candidate.

Target reader
Would be informed.

Question 5

Content (points covered)
For a Band 3 or above, the candidate's **leaflet** must:
- refer to type(s) of equipment used
- describe how they should be used
- explain procedure for emergencies.

Organisation and cohesion
Clearly organised into paragraphs.
Headings may be an advantage.

Range
Language of information and advice.
Vocabulary related to safety and equipment.

Register
Any as long as consistent.

Target reader
Would be informed.

Paper 3   English in Use (1 hour 30 minutes)

Part 1

1 B   2 D   3 A   4 C   5 A   6 C   7 A   8 A   9 A
10 D   11 B   12 C   13 D   14 A   15 C

Part 2

16 one/a/One/A   17 at   18 another   19 every/any   20 be   21 no/little
22 such   23 was   24 without   25 a/this/that   26 had
27 over/above/beyond/across   28 would   29 what   30 its

Part 3

31 Bisley   32 area are   33 However, no   34 ✓   35 well-dressing, putting
36 ✓   37 nearby   38 exhibit) and   39 religious   40 ✓   41 berries
42 into   43 pieces   44 spectacular   45 pictures   46 annual

Part 4

47 specialized/specialised   48 surgeons   49 unimaginable/unimagined
50 analysis   51 revolutionary   52 expectancy   53 increasingly
54 unreserved   55 loyalty   56 arrangements   57 appreciative   58 unbeatable
59 availability   60 savings   61 updated

Part 5

62 country/countryside 63 need/desire/want + for/on/during/from/expect + from/on
64 get it/buy it/obtain it 65 foot 66 pick up/will/may/should + get/receive
67 twice 68 for yourselves/to yourselves/for you 69 no extra/further/added/
additional 70 be available/there/waiting/present/around/meet you 71 (any)
information/advice/help 72 half(-)price/half(-)rate 73 guarantee/make sure/make
certain/be sure/be certain/ensure that 74 book now/act immediately/decide soon

Part 6

75 E 76 C 77 A 78 D 79 F 80 G

Paper 4   Listening (approximately 45 minutes)

Part 1

1 seventeenth/17th 2 nature/(the) countryside 3 status
symbol/symbol of status 4 tree planting/to plant (a) tree(s)/the planting of
trees NOT 'tree plantation' 5 (fruit and vegetable) gardens/gardening/fruit(s)
and vegetables 6 grass (land) (fields)/grasslands NOT 'fields' 7 (the)
breeding/keeping (of) (the) animals//animal breeding/animal keeping/husbandry
8 (traditional/common/contemporary) romantic (traditional)

Part 2

9 useful/of use (to people) 10 (people) blind/unable to see/not able to see 11 (big)
(large(r)) size 12 (the/some) nurses/(the/a) nurse 13 unbreakable/not breakable
14 electronic 15 (a) battery/batteries 16 response

Part 3

17 accountant 18 (rather) relieved 19 math(s)/mathematics
20 professional 21 (more) (very) supportive 22 traditional
23 drawing/to draw (like a painter) 24 abstract (art)

Part 4

25 C 26 A 27 B 28 C 29 B 30 A 31 B 32 B 33 C
34 B

Transcript   *This is the Cambridge Certificate in Advanced English Listening Test. Test Three.*

This paper requires you to listen to a selection of recorded material and answer the accompanying questions.

*There are four parts to the test. You will hear Part Two **once** only. All the other parts of the test will be heard twice.*

There will be a pause before each part to allow you to look through the questions, and other pauses to let you think about your answers. At the end of every pause you will hear this sound.

tone

*You should write your answers in the spaces provided on the **question** paper. You will have **ten minutes** at the end to **transfer your answers to the separate answer sheet.***

There will now be a pause. You must ask any questions now, as you will not be allowed to speak during the test.

[pause]

PART 1   *Now open your question paper and look at Part One.*

[pause]

You will hear a tour guide talking to a group of visitors outside an historic country house. For questions 1 to 8, complete the sentences.

You will hear the recording twice. You now have 30 seconds to look at Part One.

[pause]

tone

Tour guide: So, here we are at Newton House, a typical eighteenth-century English country house, set in its own beautiful park. Before we go inside, let's look at the park which really is a classic example of its type, with rolling grassland and scattered trees.

     Park is a word we use a lot nowadays. But if you trace back the history of the park as an idea, it is actually something which came into being as recently as the seventeenth century. People in the fifteenth and sixteenth centuries wouldn't really have understood what a park was, the idea simply didn't exist.

     But *our* ideas about the countryside have changed a lot since then too. People in past centuries knew about agriculture because most of the population was involved in it. But nature, in the sense of wild places, was seen as something dangerous. People wanted civilised, man-made landscapes that showed how the wilderness of nature could be made safe and beautiful. This was how parks began.

     Well, only rich people had parks, and socially, parkland quickly became significant as a status symbol, first appearing near large country houses like this because it was where the richest people, the big landowners, lived. Also very symbolic socially was tree-planting because trees involve long-term investment. They express a confidence in the future, and so they were carefully planted in prominent positions.

     What happened during the eighteenth century is that the park became even more important as a setting for a large house, and the fruit and vegetable gardens, which had always been attached to houses, became less significant, often hidden away to one side. This was because if the park was to clearly distinguish its owner as a wealthy person, it needed to be beautiful but not very productive.

The immediate surroundings of the house were predominantly grassland, therefore, not fields of crops; they would look too much like work. But that doesn't mean that the land was completely useless. Rich people often involved themselves in breeding animals, for example, which was regarded as a kind of acceptable form of agriculture, something more like a sport.

Later, in the nineteenth century, urban parks appeared, taking up some of the ideas of rural park design, and those coming from Romantic traditions, common at the time, of what represented the picturesque. These pretty corners in cities gradually came to be used for the recreation of growing urban populations. This was quite a different purpose from that of the country park, which could be seen as representing a kind of barrier around the rich who were increasingly wanting to distance themselves from local farming communities, as well as from the growing urban areas.

[pause]

tone

Now you will hear the recording again.

[The recording is repeated.]

[pause]

That is the end of Part One.

[pause]

PART 2

Part Two

You will hear the winner of a competition for young inventors talking about her invention. For questions 9 to 16, complete the sentences.

*Listen very carefully as you will hear the recording **once** only. You now have 45 seconds to look at Part Two.*

[pause]

tone

Presenter: Our guest today is Sonia Reed, winner of a competition for young inventors. Sonia, tell us about your invention.

Sonia: Thank you. Well, the judges in the competition were looking for a new invention that would be both useful and commercially viable. Although I knew my invention was of use to people, I'd never thought about the commercial possibilities, so winning was a lovely surprise.

Briefly, my invention is a medical thermometer for blind people. Basically, it differs from a normal thermometer in that it makes a noise, which I thought would be useful for people who are not able to see. For a temperature of 37 degrees, which is normal, it gives one beep, and then two beeps for 38 degrees and three for 39 degrees.

People have been surprised that it only has three signals, but actually human temperature varies very little and so that's really all that's necessary. The aspect that I'm less happy with is the noise itself. It would be better if the thermometer could speak, like some watches can. It could say something like 'forty degrees – see a doctor immediately'. But to do that, it would have to be much bigger and I wanted to keep it about the same size as an ordinary thermometer.

It still has various advantages over the conventional thermometer, actually, even for sighted people. Firstly, in hospitals, nurses take people's temperatures, but don't always tell them what it is, they just whip it away, which worries people. With one that makes a noise, everyone knows what the situation is, even in the absence of a doctor.

And of course, it's good for all sorts of other reasons. It's unbreakable and there is nothing poisonous in it. The idea first came to me actually when I was feeling unwell. I dropped a glass thermometer which smashed and the mercury inside, which is poisonous of course, splashed all over the floor. I started to think that thermometers really had a lot of disadvantages. That's when I had the idea that maybe an electronic sensor could be used to record the temperature. That's where my colleague Colin came in. He advised me about the best kind of electronic circuit to use.

Some people are worried that all this bleeping may disturb patients in hospitals, but we don't think so because it switches itself off after five seconds. If it didn't, people might leave it on and the battery would run down very quickly. As it is, the power will last for a very long time indeed, so you don't have to keep on buying a new battery for it. And, as a result of Colin's design, you get what I call 'an immediate response'. You don't have to sit there for ages with it in your mouth waiting for the mercury to react.

Now, if there are any questions.

[pause]

That is the end of Part Two.

[pause]

PART 3

Part Three

You will hear part of an interview with a sculptor who is talking about his life and work. For questions 17 to 24, complete the sentences.

You will hear the recording twice. You now have one minute to look at Part Three.

[pause]

tone

Interviewer: My guest today is the artist, Alan Carey, who over the last thirty years has established himself as one of this country's leading sculptors, making a range of fascinating objects out of metal, stone and other materials. Alan, welcome.
Alan Carey: Hello.
Interviewer: But you don't come from an artistic background, do you, Alan?
Alan Carey: Oh, absolutely not. If my father had had anything to do with it, I'd never have gone in for sculpture because he was an accountant and ideally he wanted me to join his firm, or if not, go into insurance or banking. But none of these ideas

appealed to me, I'm afraid. I'd been doing sculpture as a hobby through my teenage years and, although my parents encouraged me in that, it didn't seem like a prospective career at the time, at least not to my father.

Interviewer: But he got a sculptor to look at your work at one point, didn't he?

Alan Carey: Oddly enough, yes. We went to see a man who taught sculpture in a big London art school who said, 'Well, let's have a look at the work', and this chap looked at it and said to my father, 'Your son will never be any good, you know', and my father was rather relieved and said to me, 'You see, you can do it as a hobby'. And then, when we got home he said, 'Well, what *do* you want to do?' and I didn't know … engineering? … architecture? I considered various things, even geology, but finally, in the end, after I'd got a maths degree, I said, 'What I really want to do is sculpture, you know' and he said, 'Well, you'd better do it then'.

Interviewer: So, he gave in, in the end?

Alan Carey: He did. But I'm glad it happened that way, that I had to struggle to do it, because he made me dedicate myself to sculpture and do the job properly. He had the idea that art was for amateurs, and that was the one thing that I did not want to be. I wanted to do it as a professional. I knew he was wrong, so I set out to prove it. And, you know, I'm sure that if I had joined his firm, I'd have done it in a half-hearted way which he wouldn't have approved of anyway. And I must say, after I'd decided to become a sculptor, he couldn't have been more supportive.

Interviewer: And so you went on to art college. Did you enjoy it?

Alan Carey: At the beginning, I appreciated it a lot because we had a different teacher every term. This meant you got a good grounding in the basics because you picked up different things from each one, you know, it might be the material they worked in, for example, or their technique, or whatever. But eventually I got fairly restless because it was a five-year course and by about half-way through I was getting a bit fed up because it was extremely traditional in terms of approach and I was looking for something more out of the ordinary.

Interviewer: So this was what led you to Harold Morton?

Alan Carey: Yes, he was the most advanced sculptor of the time, he was really doing very different things which I found exciting. And so I sent him some photos of my work, on the off-chance, and amazingly he offered me a part-time job and so I managed to combine that with the final years of college, which made all the difference.

Interviewer: And how would you sum up that experience, what did you get out of it?

Alan Carey: Well, we talked about art a lot. He taught me that a sculptor's studio is quite different from art college. I had to do drawing at college, a subject I never really understood, and when I got back, he would criticise what I'd done. And from him, I learnt how a sculptor draws, because I was being taught by painters, who are looking at things in a different way.

Interviewer: And I suppose it was thanks to him that you started doing abstract art?

Alan Carey: Well, yes it was, because I don't do sculptures of people or animals, they're not meant to be lifelike. So they are examples of what, I suppose, you'd call abstract art. They are meant to mean something, to make you think.

Interviewer: But you give them titles, don't you? Why?

Alan Carey: Well, the titles get attached to them later ...

[pause]

tone

Now you will hear the recording again.

[The recording is repeated.]

[pause]

That is the end of Part Three.

[pause]

PART 4   *Now look at the fourth and last part of the test.*

You will hear five short extracts in which different people are talking about living in a village. Each extract has two questions. For questions 25 to 34, choose the correct answer A, B or C.

You will hear the recording twice. You now have one minute to look at Part Four.

[pause]

tone

Speaker One: The town's noisy and filthy and I couldn't live there, though the entertainment's good, whereas it's pretty quiet here. But it's a major expedition to get into town to meet my friends. The local council have 'upgraded' our service so there's a regular bus, which sounds good, doesn't it? Yes, well it <u>is</u> regular – once a day instead of once a week. And midday's no good for the disco, is it? And It's a huge double-decker with three or four on board, if you're lucky. No, we need something different, something much smaller which could also be booked for special journeys if people wanted, perhaps owned and run by the community itself?

Speaker Two: There used to be quite a lot going on, agriculture and small firms, traditional country crafts mainly. Now the farms are suffering and laying off workers, and city people are buying up cottages so rising house prices are hitting the little enterprises. And people are giving up and drifting away. These are hard times, but I'm not sure we're doing enough. We should be taking the future into our own hands, finding finance for things we want by taking advantage of any government schemes, like this public-private partnership idea for instance, to set up new ventures or expand existing concerns so the young can stay in the countryside. After all, technology is on our side now, isn't it?

Speaker Three: I'm thinking of moving into the town. It's manageable here with a car, but running one now is so dear and I'm not getting any younger. What will I do when I'm reduced to public transport, that'll be fun, won't it? My granddaughter says 'shop on the Internet', if I can learn how to use a computer at my age! I don't think it's fair that we should pay the same for petrol as they do in town where they've got buses and underground. We need a more flexible system, special rates for the countryside. Then we could afford to keep our cars and help our neighbours who haven't got their own transport.

171

Speaker Four: I like living here. I work from home – computer technology and e-mail have changed life completely. No commuting, no waiting at draughty bus stops any more! But what can you do in your spare time? – chat to friends in the pub? You can walk or cycle for exercise but that's not very social, is it? I'd like something for team games – nothing much, a pitch with a club house. There's some land we could use, but it'll need effort and some cash. The local council might help with a grant or a loan and we could supply the labour. It would bring the youth together, give them somewhere to go.

Speaker Five: My husband works in the town and we can't afford two cars so I'm stuck here all day. There's still a primary school for the kids but the grocer's gone and the post office is threatened with closure and then what'll I do? I think it's partly our own fault. We all go to the town when we can and so we're not making use of what's here in the village. Perhaps we should be more conscious of the community. I wouldn't mind helping to get a grocer's off the ground or start a mobile one. It might be fun learning how to do that.

[pause]

tone

Now you will hear the recording again. Remember you must complete both tasks.

[The recording is repeated.]

[pause]

*That is the end of Part Four. There will now be a ten-minute pause to allow you to **transfer your answers to the separate answer sheet.** Be sure to follow the numbering of all the questions. The question papers and answer sheets will then be collected by your supervisor.*

[Teacher, pause the recording here for ten minutes. Remind your students when they have one minute left.]

That is the end of the test.

Test 4 Key

Paper 1   Reading (1 hour 15 minutes)

Part 1

1 E   2 C   3 D   4 F   5 B   6 F   7 C   8 B   9 D
10 A   11 E   12 C   13 F   14 A   15 B

Part 2

16 F   17 D   18 G   19 E   20 A   21 C

Part 3

22 C   23 C   24 A   25 A   26 D   27 D   28 B

Part 4

29 C   30 E   31 A   32 D   33 E   34 D   35 B   36 A
37 C   38 D   39 B   40 A   41 E   42 C   43 B   44 E
45 D

Paper 2   Writing (2 hours)

Task-specific mark scheme

Part 1

Question 1

Content (points covered)
For Band 3 or above, the candidate's **letter** must:
• thank manager for invitation to Arts Centre
• comment on positive points of Arts Centre
• explain why writer was disappointed
• suggest meeting.

Organisation and cohesion
Clear paragraphs. Letter layout with opening and closing formulae.

Range
Language of evaluation, explanation and suggestion.

Register
Formal to unmarked. Not aggressive.

Target reader
Would be informed and would consider meeting to discuss issues.

Part 2

Question 2

Content (points covered)
For Band 3 or above, the candidate's **article** must:
• mention the impact of mobile phones
• mention at least one type/example of **both** personal **and** business use
• refer to advantages **and** disadvantages of mobile phones.

Organisation and cohesion
Clear organisation with appropriate paragraphing and linking devices.

Range
Language of description. Vocabulary related to mobile phones.

Register
May mix register if appropriate to approach taken by candidate.

Target reader
Would be informed.

Question 3

Content (points covered)
For Band 3 or above, the candidate's **proposal** must:
• persuade reader that town is suitable for event
• comment on
  – accommodation
  – transport
  – entertainment.

Organisation and cohesion
Clearly paragraphed.

Range
Language of description, evaluation and persuasion.

Register
Consistently formal or unmarked.

Target reader
Would be informed.

Question 4

Content (points covered)
For Band 3 or above, the candidate's **text for the leaflet** must refer to:
• methods of study
• accommodation
• social life.

Organisation and cohesion
Clear sections or paragraphs.
Headings may be an advantage.

Range
Vocabulary of school and study.

Register
Any as long as consistent.

Target reader
Would be informed.

Question 5

Content (points covered)
For Band 3 or above, the candidate's **report** must:
- describe experience at trade fair
- recommend company's attendance next year.

Organisation and cohesion
Clearly organised in paragraphs.
Headings may be an advantage.

Range
Language of description and persuasion. Business vocabulary.

Register
Any as long as consistent.

Target reader
Would be informed.

Paper 3   English in Use (1 hour 30 minutes)

Part 1

1 A   2 A   3 D   4 C   5 D   6 D   7 A   8 B   9 A
10 C   11 A   12 C   13 B   14 D   15 A

Part 2

16 all   17 in   18 but/only/yet   19 them   20 or/nor   21 his
22 where/when   23 and   24 with/for   25 to   26 there
27 it   28 had/Had/has/Has   29 too   30 although

Part 3

31 Earth :/;/,/-   32 changes to   33 accompanied   34 physicists
35 observations   36 interruption   37 ✓   38 360 years   39 ✓
40 behaviour/behavior   41 Australia   42 said, 'I   43 eclipse.' Joanna/eclipse'.
Joanna   44 ✓   45 emerged   46 Sun's

Part 4

47 monotonous   **48** adaptation   **49** elegance   **50** excellent   **51** sympathetic
52 complexity   **53** remarkable   **54** archaeological/archeological
55 significance   **56** recognition   **57** R/responsibilities
58 computerisation/computerization   **59** accessibility   **60** appointments
61 educational/education

Part 5

62 professional   **63** adapted/adjusted/altered/(re) arranged/(re)organised/modified/
changed/laid out   **64** begin/commence/open/start + (with)   **65** collection/combination/
compilation/range/variety   **66** agreement   **67** his/the + final/last/senior
68 critical/crucial/important/pressing/notable/serious   **69** a little/fairly/quite/rather
70 acting/performance   **71** last long   **72** amusing/funny/humorous
73 entire/whole   **74** be remembered

Part 6

75 G   **76** C   **77** D   **78** H   **79** A   **80** F

Paper 4   Listening (approximately 45 minutes)

Part 1

1 Far Horizons/far horizons   **2** alone/on your own
3 tools/equipment/(you need)   **4** above freezing/above 0°C (centigrade)/above
zero   **5** (effective) (some) heating/heat   **6** (enormous) tree trunks ACCEPT
trunks   **7** polar bear(s)   **8** (a) package tour(s)/(a) package
holiday(s)/(tourist) packages/a package

Part 2

9 open homes/Open Homes   **10** pen(-)friend/pen(-)pal   **11** (foreign) (other) (their)
languages/a language/a foreign language/another language NOT the language(s)
12 France/Germany ANY ORDER   **13** loneliness/feeling lonely
14 (professional) (group) leader   **15** fun/entertainment/entertaining   **16** wild(-)life

Part 3

17 A   **18** B   **19** D   **20** D   **21** C   **22** B   **23** A

Part 4

24 G   **25** A   **26** D   **27** F   **28** B   **29** D   **30** C   **31** H   **32** B
33 F

Transcript

This is the Cambridge Certificate in Advanced English Listening Test. Test Four.

This paper requires you to listen to a selection of recorded material and answer the accompanying questions.

*There are four parts to the test. You will hear Part Two **once** only. All the other parts of the test will be heard twice.*

There will be a pause before each part to allow you to look through the questions, and other pauses to let you think about your answers. At the end of every pause you will hear this sound.

tone

*You should write your answers in the spaces provided on the **question** paper. You will have **ten** minutes at the end to **transfer your answers to the separate answer sheet.***

There will now be a pause. You must ask any questions now, as you will not be allowed to speak during the test.

[pause]

PART 1

Now open your question paper and look at Part One.

[pause]

You will hear a journalist called Peter Smith talking about a trip he made to the Arctic seas around the North Pole. For questions 1 to 8, complete the sentences.

You will hear the recording twice. You now have 30 seconds to look at Part One.

[pause]

tone

Peter Smith: I can't pinpoint the exact moment when I made the decision to embark on my sailing expedition to the North Pole. The previous summer I'd come across a book entitled *Far Horizons* which suggested that a voyage of this kind was a unique experience – and everyone should try it once! So, I put on three layers of clothing and set off in my boat in July with a small crew to sail to the Arctic seas near the North Pole. I felt it was time I went in search of adventure!

I'd been told that sailing there shouldn't present any more problems than you'd expect sailing round the seas in the north of Britain. Well, initially that was true. But there were differences. The most noticeable is that, up there in the Arctic seas, you have the impression of being alone. So, if anything breaks down or goes wrong – for example, one of our large front cabin windows shattered in the gale we encountered on our first night – you have to have all the tools you need. We would have been very cold and wet if we hadn't had the means to make a solid repair. The second big difference is the temperature. In the winter in those seas, things can get down to minus fifty degrees. In the summer, it's much warmer and the surface sea water is always above freezing but the air temperature never rises much above ten degrees. This all means two things. The first is that the cabin of your boat must have effective heating. The second is that you must have proper outdoor clothing. Another difference is that you meet some things that aren't found on a normal sailing trip. Not surprisingly, we met gigantic lumps of ice which had broken off icebergs, and occasionally we saw enormous tree trunks on the sea. We really weren't sure what they were doing there!

They do say that in those seas you can even spot polar bears, which are reported to be very dangerous if disturbed. Unfortunately, we weren't able to catch sight of one, although we did see whales.

For all this effort, though, you're rewarded with a trip to a true wilderness, which can be reached in your very own boat. More than 250,000 tourists visit this area each year, but in order to protect the environment, and because of the difficulty in getting there, most of the tourism takes the form of package tours. These have only limited access to certain unrestricted areas. But, in your own boat, you can have the whole area to yourself!

[pause]

tone

Now you will hear the recording again.

[The recording is repeated.]

[pause]

That is the end of Part One.

[pause]

PART 2

Part Two

You will hear the headteacher of a school talking to a group of parents about an international student exchange programme. For questions 9 to 16, complete the sentences.

*Listen very carefully as you will hear the recording **once** only. You now have 45 seconds to look at Part Two.*

[pause]

tone

Headteacher: Good evening, I'd like to welcome all those parents whose children have just started at the school. The purpose of this meeting is to give you information about the international exchange programme known as 'Open Homes', which the school runs. For one week a year, pupils are invited to stay with a family abroad and attend school with a child the same age. A return visit is then arranged six months later, when our pupils and their families open their homes and become the hosts.

In general, children aged thirteen to fifteen-years-old, but no younger, seem to get something out of this trip. Now, I realise that your own children will only be eleven or at most twelve this year, but we feel that it's important to begin by making the links that will make a future exchange more successful. So we want children to make a penfriend of their prospective overseas partners a year or so before the visit. By taking part in this scheme, they will already know someone in, and a lot about, their destination before they leave.

We've established links with schools in various countries. In the past, European exchanges have been the most popular, especially amongst children keen to practise their languages. But this is not the only aim of the programme, so those more interested in other subjects should not be put off. One year, we organised a trip to Holland which was very successful, although none of the children were studying Dutch. Our most regular destination, however, is France, with Germany coming a close second, although we are in touch with a school in Poland which is very keen to take part, as is a school in Canada.

Although most children love the experience, we must be prepared for some difficulties. This may be the child's first trip abroad, leading to feelings of homesickness as well as loneliness. A week can seem a long time when you feel lonely or you're missing home. So each group of pupils is accompanied by a professional group leader, which means there's always someone with training on the spot to solve any difficulties, which is a relief for both parents and host families as you can imagine.

There is variety built in the week and this definitely helps. For example, children attend lessons together in the morning and then visit a local place of interest in the afternoon. These trips can be fun as well as educationally valuable and parents are invited to come along too. In the past we've managed to combine the pure entertainment of places like theme parks with the learning opportunities provided by wildlife parks, museums, etc. And surprisingly, it's actually the wildlife rather than the theme parks which prove the most popular time and time again.

So I hope I've given you ...

[pause]

That is the end of Part Two.

[pause]

PART 3

Part Three

You will hear part of an interview with Norman Cowley, a well-known novelist and biographer. For questions 17 to 23, choose the correct answer A, B, C or D.

You will hear the recording twice. You now have one minute to look at Part Three.

[pause]

tone

Interviewer: With us today to discuss his career we have Norman Cowley, renowned novelist and biographer. So let's start at the beginning, Norman. You did say, some years ago, that you began high on the mountain, only to go down sharply while others were passing you on the way up. Do you think now, when you look back at your first novel, that it had anything that you were not able to recapture later?

Norman Cowley:	You can't write a worthwhile book, or you can't continue to be a reasonable writer if you start recapturing what you've done earlier. So there are all sorts of positive things in my first book that I'll never achieve again – the immediacy of it, the easiness of the dialogue, the kind of stylistic elegance that comes from not trying to be too sophisticated. But, on the other hand, I wouldn't want to repeat it.
Interviewer:	Now, after the tremendous success of that first novel, your second one was pretty much damned by the critics.
Norman Cowley:	Oh, more than damned. It was torn apart!
Interviewer:	Well, now, that must have hurt, probably more than anything subsequently.
Norman Cowley:	It was shocking, because, and you know this is going to sound silly, but I couldn't believe the intensity of the attack on it. I remember one awful review by a longstanding, distinguished critic, who was uncharacteristically attempting to be witty, I suspect. He wrote that the book was 'paceless, tasteless, graceless'. Now it certainly had its faults but er … it had pace, it had its own kind of taste in tune with the youth culture of the time, and I like to think it had some grace. It was almost as if the reviewer had deliberately set out to pick the few good things he could find in the book and wreck them too. It was a demolition job.
Interviewer:	But did this rejection push you in a different direction?
Norman Cowley:	It left me very confused. I thought maybe I should give up and become something else, but I didn't know what. So I wandered around and finally started thinking about the next book, 'The Green Wood'. Of course you get good reviews too, which give you hope, and the bad ones toughen you. Finally after many, many years, you realise that it's part of it. In a way, it's a pruning process. It cuts down all but the people who are really driven to be writers. So there are far more people who write two novels than six or seven.
Interviewer:	After a while, people began to see some autobiographical content in your fiction. Was that fair?
Norman Cowley:	It was half fair. You don't ever put someone into a book completely. You don't dare because if you do, you've got a dull character. The point is that if you put people that you know very well, like your wife or children, into a book, they're real for you already, so you don't have to create them. So they say a few things that they say every day and they're real for you, but not for anyone else. It's better if you change them. I love taking people and transforming them to a degree by, say, putting them in an occupation they don't have and so on.
Interviewer:	And what do you think about some of the novels written today with their extremely violent plots?
Norman Cowley:	I don't care what characters do in a novel. I'm willing to read about the worst human monster, provided the novelist can make that person come alive. A novel should enable you to learn more about the depths of human nature. Some of today's violent novels don't do that. There's no inner voyage. The writing's descriptive but not revealing. Probably there's such a thing as 'going too far', but only if you don't fulfil the prescription. You can go as far as you want but your imagination has to be equal to it.
Interviewer:	So the novel is still mainly a kind of psychological journey?
Norman Cowley:	Well, it can be many things: a riddle, a game or a wonderful revolution of language. I would hate to say novels have to be <u>one</u> thing, but the key is that they should illuminate human experience in a dramatic way. Otherwise why read them? You're going to get a better, swiftly-paced, modern narrative on the average TV show.

Interviewer:	Now, in your selection of subjects for biographical treatment, is there one aspect of all these people which attracted you?
Norman Cowley:	Well, yes, I feel that I'm in a position to write biographies of people who are well-known, not necessarily because I'm as large a celebrity as they are, although I do think I have more insight into them than the average good, worthy biographer. They approach from the outside and don't understand the incredible confusion of identities that grows when you come to celebrity from simpler beginnings. That's what draws me to these people. Also you have the great advantage of knowing what happened. When you're a novelist … you panic about what to do next. You could wreck the book if you go the wrong way.
Interviewer:	Now let's turn to your latest novel, which has …

[pause]

tone

Now you will hear the recording again.

[The recording is repeated.]

[pause]

That is the end of Part Three.

[pause]

PART 4　　*Now look at the fourth and last part of the test. Part Four consists of two tasks.*

You will hear five short extracts in which different people are talking about the means of escape they use to cope with the demands of their working lives. Look at Task One. For questions 24 to 28, match the extracts with what each speaker finds demanding about their work, listed A to H. Now look at Task Two. For questions 29 to 33, match the extracts with what attracts the speakers to their different means of escape, listed A to H.

You will hear the recording twice and while you listen you must complete both tasks. You now have 40 seconds to look at Part Four.

[pause]

tone

Speaker One:	I enjoy speed in every walk of life. Perhaps it's my weakness but I feel that time's so precious you mustn't waste it. That's why my car's my means of escape. I've always loved the sense of danger when driving fast cars and, if I didn't own the transport company I work in, I'd probably be a racing driver! The trouble is that because of the company's high profile, I'm often recognised. Now that's where the car comes in. I rarely take passengers or use it for any practical purpose. I just get in it and drive for hours. When I'm old and grey, I don't want to have any regrets. I don't want to think I didn't take advantage of the opportunities life offered me!
Speaker Two:	The garden was a wilderness when we moved into our present house. As a youngster, I'd always wanted a tree house in the garden and now it seems that I've built the deluxe version. It stands on stilts in the corner of the garden

181

where nothing would grow. It even has a balcony and a light inside it! I don't know what I'd do if I didn't have it to escape to. You see, being an opera singer is an athletic pursuit and you have to train like an athlete for it. Once I get on stage, I'm swept along by the sheer feeling of commitment I have to what I do. You have to have access to grand passions to be able to live the part … which is great, but the need to switch off is even greater.

Speaker Three: I've been going to watch Rugby football for over 25 years now. The club is totally amateur. There are no spectator stands and it's absolutely freezing in winter. The crowds vary between two and three hundred, though, depending on the fixture. But as soon as I walk into the ground, I completely switch off from the day-to-day pressure of the bank where I work as managing director – even if the game gets a bit lively sometimes! You see, I believe team games give you a better insight into what life is all about: that you have to take the knocks as well as give them, and that you can achieve more by working together than you can as an individual.

Speaker Four: My means of escape isn't a solitary place. It's the study area part of our first floor living room and, with five-year-old twins and four older children, it's what you might call a place with quite a lot of hubbub. I sit here at the end of a long day and drink tea. Everyone near and dear to me comes in and out and talks about what they've been doing. My days are always busy because I work as a consultant in a hospital and every Tuesday I have a special clinic in the evenings, so I'm absolutely worn out most of the time. It's being at home that enables me to recharge my batteries.

Speaker Five: There's a ranch in the US which I love going to. You ride in the morning in groups according to your ability and in the afternoons there are lawn games or whatever. You live in small cabins, which are comfortable rather than luxurious, and you eat good, plain food. It's so different from being a chief executive of an oil company, and I find it really relaxing. You see, when the company was originally founded in 1886, it took four months to get a message from the Far East. Now people are checking the stock market every two seconds and asking what you're going to do about so-and-so. Soon everything will be screened directly into your brain. You'll close your eyes and see the price of shares!

[pause]

tone

Now you will hear the recording again. Remember you must complete both tasks.

[The recording is repeated.]

[pause]

That is the end of Part Four. There will now be a ten-minute pause to allow you to **transfer your answers to the separate answer sheet.** *Be sure to follow the numbering of all the questions. The question papers and answer sheets will then be collected by your supervisor.*

[Teacher, pause the recording here for ten minutes. Remind your students when they have one minute left.]

That is the end of the test.

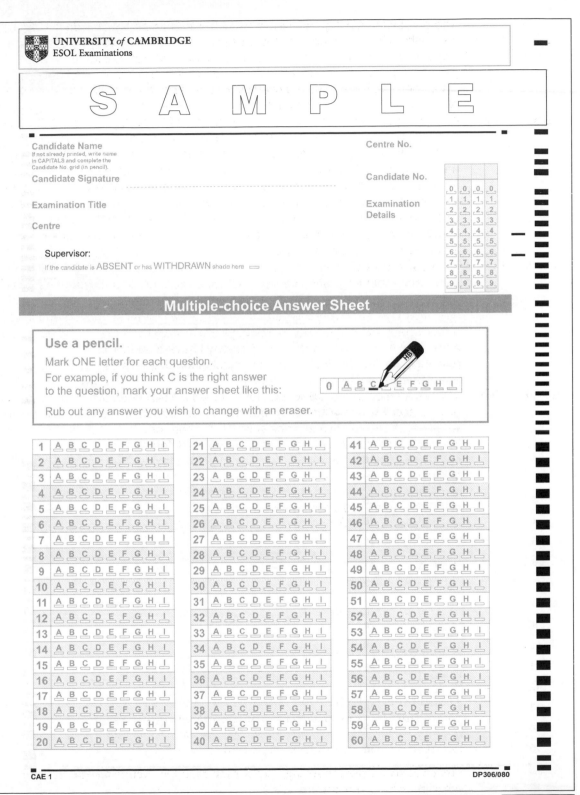

Sample answer sheet: Paper 3

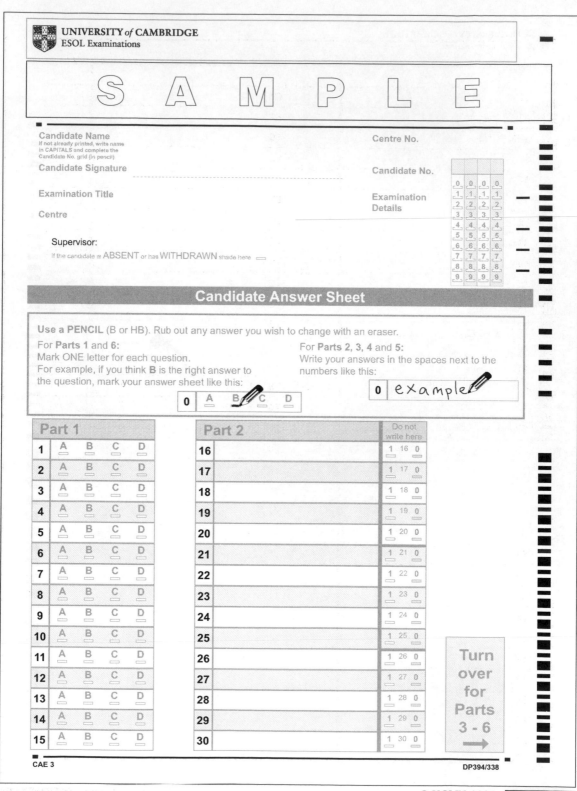

Part 3

		Do not write here
31		1 31 0
32		1 32 0
33		1 33 0
34		1 34 0
35		1 35 0
36		1 36 0
37		1 37 0
38		1 38 0
39		1 39 0
40		1 40 0
41		1 41 0
42		1 42 0
43		1 43 0
44		1 44 0
45		1 45 0
46		1 46 0

Part 4

		Do not write here
47		1 47 0
48		1 48 0
49		1 49 0
50		1 50 0
51		1 51 0
52		1 52 0
53		1 53 0
54		1 54 0
55		1 55 0
56		1 56 0
57		1 57 0
58		1 58 0
59		1 59 0
60		1 60 0
61		1 61 0

Part 5

		Do not write here
62		1 62 0
63		1 63 0
64		1 64 0
65		1 65 0
66		1 66 0
67		1 67 0
68		1 68 0
69		1 69 0
70		1 70 0
71		1 71 0
72		1 72 0
73		1 73 0
74		1 74 0

Part 6

	A	B	C	D	E	F	G	H	I
75	A	B	C	D	E	F	G	H	I
76	A	B	C	D	E	F	G	H	I
77	A	B	C	D	E	F	G	H	I
78	A	B	C	D	E	F	G	H	I
79	A	B	C	D	E	F	G	H	I
80	A	B	C	D	E	F	G	H	I

Sample answer sheet: Paper 4

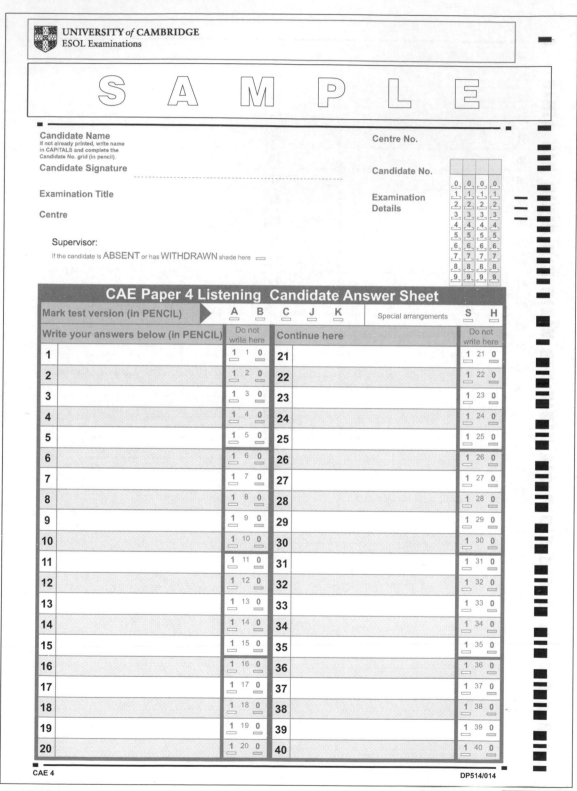